DIVINE
THINGS

DIVINE THINGS

SEEKING THE SACRED IN A SECULAR AGE

ROBERT KIRSCHNER

A Crossroad Book
The Crossroad Publishing Company
New York

The Crossroad Publishing Company
481 Eighth Avenue, New York, NY 10001

Printed in the United States of America

Library of Congress Cataloging-in-Publication Data
Kirschner, Robert (Robert S.)
     Divine things : seeking the sacred in a secular age / by Robert Kirschner.
       p. cm.
     ISBN 0-8245-1897-7 (alk. paper)
     1. Faith (Judaism) 2. Revelation (Jewish theology) 3. Judaism and science. 4. Ethics, Jewish. 5. Jewish way of life. I. Title.
BM729.F3 K57 2000
296.3 – dc21

                                                            00-011413

1   2   3   4   5   6   7   8   9   10   06   05   04   03   02   01

He never supposed
That he might be truth, himself, or part of it,
That the things that he rejected might be part
And the irregular turquoise, part, the perceptible blue
Grown denser, part, the eye so touched, so played
Upon by clouds, the ear so magnified
By thunder, part, and all these things together,
Parts, and more things, parts. He never supposed divine
Things might not look divine, nor that if nothing
Was divine then all things were...

—Wallace Stevens
from "Landscape with Boat"

Contents

divine things

TRUTH, OR PART OF IT

IT HAS BEEN SAID that religion is a profound response to a question that no one is asking anymore. As a rabbi, I have often felt that way. In our days, theological language is rarely heard outside the house of worship; and inside, the empty seats testify to its decline. Even for those still there, the creeds of past ages cross our tongues with difficulty. The mind rarely assents, and the heart is unmoved. In the synagogues that I have known, most Jews regard themselves as visitors. The rituals are viewed as exotic; the Scriptures seem as relevant as the Rosetta stone. Hebrew prayers are pronounced phonetically, without comprehension. There is sound but no fury.

The fixed forms of religion, whether institutional or intellectual, have their valued place. Any architecture requires some rigidity if it is to endure. The Temple of ancestral faith still stands. But in a secular culture where so many live at a spiritual distance, that faith must depart the holy precincts. It must find its way in hard and stony territory, where science and empiricism prevail, where religion is equated with delusion and faith with superstition. It must reckon with a view of life that, like Darwin's theory, discerns growth and change but denies given destinies. It must find, in its frayed lexicon, a repertoire of concepts that can survive translation from ancient to modern, from sacred to secular. It must create a shared idiom, forged of acquaintance with truths old and new, one that does not regard these as incommensurate.

Accustomed to privileging our moment in time above all the others, regarding it as the culmination of wisdom, we often condescend to the past. We act as if our conclusions automatically supersede all of the previous ones. Having long ago exposed the fallacy of scriptural inerrancy, we attribute the same perfection to modern forms of knowledge. We act as if scientific discourse has finally explained reality, when in truth it is no more intelligible to most of us than the spells of a sorcerer.

To proclaim, with Nietzsche, the death of God, is another uniquely modern conceit. It discards the verdict of a hundred generations: the truths they found, the moral standards they accepted, the transcendent purposes they sought. Beyond the flux of chance and circumstance, argues Nietzsche, there is only the abyss. It is as if the Bible is now to be read backward, ending, rather than beginning, with the void.

But if the Bible is read in the other direction, in sympathy if not in conformity with the past, we find that it still has a story, indeed many stories, to tell. The Hebrew Scriptures blink at us, like quasars, from a galactic distance. Their ghostly light is not always strong enough to reach us or bright enough to guide our way. But even across the vast expanse, their radiance still registers. When light travels that far, surely it has something to teach us.

Jews call the first five books of the Bible the Torah, a Hebrew word for "instruction," referring to the divine commandments. Over the centuries the Jewish sages have infused every word of the Torah with a sublime valence. Many of their deductions and interpretations are found in this book. One need not share their conviction to appreciate their labors. Like us, they sought the eternal verities with the instruments at hand; for their voyage of faith, the Torah was compass, map, and plumb line. As the clamorous rabbinic commentaries attest, the sages were more prone to argument than to resolution. But it was the argument that enthralled them.

Progress toward the apprehension of God's will, however halting, was their share of revelation, as if they too stood with Moses at Sinai.

When we listen to Scripture and sage, we gain more than mere access to the past. We are also granted respite from the tyranny of the present. The electronic culture has conditioned us to the immediate at the expense of the perennial. Our daily newspapers publish morning, afternoon, and evening editions. Various television and radio stations broadcast nothing but news. On the worldwide web, communication is instantaneous. The importance of events becomes a function of how recently they happened. But as the momentary replaces the abiding, so the petty obstructs the profound, much as, in the Hasidic image, a finger held to the eye can block the sun.

Instant communication has exacted another price: the acuity of our perceptions. On the one hand, our sensory capacities have been greatly expanded. X-rays and CAT scans, electron microscopes and radio telescopes have exceeded the limits of mortal vision. We have beheld the earth from beyond its own atmosphere. We hear voices from places we have never been and people we will never see. Information pours in through every channel and medium: light waves, air waves, telephone cables, and printing presses. Yet on the other hand, our senses have shriveled. So incessant and insistent is the influx of data that the circuits overload; reception shuts down. It has been argued that communication technology is actually altering the human sensorium, replacing sustained attention with momentary image, linear thought with random sequence. One of modern life's anomalies is that our technology has steadily distanced us from physical contact with reality: we have literally taken leave of our senses. The devices designed to surpass our faculties have numbed them. The mind, as one writer has said, is more and more like a lonely and immobile monarch, immured in the throne room of the skull, unable to rely upon his messengers.

Here, too, the ancients can help us. More intimately acquainted with sensory reality, more vulnerable to the abrasions of the natural world, they can awaken us to perceptions that have atrophied. Resonating to a music we rarely hear, they can serve as a kind of tuning fork, disclosing the forgotten pitch of the spirit.

A depersonalized, technological world can diminish the spiritual dimension of life, but it cannot extinguish it. Granting the modern preoccupation with the here and now, there is still a yearning for a more exalted perspective, one less concerned with the timely than with the timeless. Despite the secular culture's steady diet of confections, there is still a hunger for bread. Notwithstanding the flood of the strident and superficial, there is still a thirst for sincerity. The proliferation of data has not stilled these yearnings. Neither the computer nor the cellular phone has changed the fact of mortality or the want of wisdom. Ultimate truths know no chronological criteria and cannot be confused with fashion.

One of the most ancient Jewish customs is to sound the shofar, a ram's horn, in the synagogue at the Jewish New Year. The purpose is to summon the community to reflection and repentance. Anyone who has heard the blast of the shofar would not call it music. It is more like a cry, a shriek, a ululation. Some years ago, several Jewish congregations of innovative temper decided that it was time to update the ritual. They replaced the ram's horn with a trumpet. They assumed that a more advanced instrument would produce a more pleasing sound. But the experiment failed: people preferred the distressing shriek of the primitive horn. Effortless technology and predictability cannot always replace the primal and the simple. Jews have learned that the shrill and broken notes of the shofar are truer to life.

You can never understand one language, John Searle has written, unless you understand two. Jews have never existed in a vacuum but in symbiosis with the prevailing culture.

The link between the two has been enriched by their differences. Perspective is conferred by incongruity: each gains in definition exactly as it diverges from, rather than resembles, the other. Between the trumpet and the shofar is a spiritual and chronological gulf. Yet the gulf is also a bridge: we learn from their dissonance what we cannot learn from their harmony. We learn from Scripture what we cannot learn from science. We learn from our senses what we cannot learn from machines. We learn from the heart what the mind cannot tell us.

How, without forfeiting modern insights, to learn anew the ancient ones: that is the project of this book. Its perspective is the Jewish religious tradition; its angle of vision is that of a modern rabbi; yet the horizon it seeks is an open one. The religion described in these pages is not a finished product. It is an avowal of the divine, not a proof of it. It seeks to differ from works of theology that sound as if the author walked all the way around God and took pictures. Here there is no claim to privileged insight. In lieu of the knowledge of God, this book offers occasions of belief and of doubt, of reverie and of wakefulness. It offers the Jewish tradition as an inherited version of experience to compare to one's own.

When I speak of Jewish tradition, I mean to cast a wide net. Judaism is less a religious doctrine than a historical phenomenon, singular in ancestry but plural in expression. Like a helix, it spirals through the life of the Jewish people, at once shaping and shaped by their trials and their tenacity. Categorical definitions of Judaism have proven elusive; the classical rabbinic works are not inclined toward unanimity and refuse to impose consensus. The story is told of an Anglican scholar who planned to lecture on "The Systematic Theology of the Synagogue," only to be informed by a refractory Jew: "First of all, there is no official Synagogue; and if there were, it wouldn't have a theology; and if it did, it wouldn't be systematic." On the other hand, there is no mistaking the singularity of the Torah and its rabbinic elaboration, or the grand spiritual mansion that has been raised on their foundation. These pages propose to offer a tour of its rooms.

The itinerary is a modest one, preferring brief visits to long sojourns, and economy to expense. The compression of the essays reflects a particular cast of mind. I have always felt an affinity for the astringent forms of literature, from biblical psalm to rabbinic aphorism, from poem to short story. I appreciate these not only for their succinctness but for their focus, their refusal to digress. They achieve their greatest power when each line is a signal, each word an arrow. Of course, I cannot claim such art for these essays. But if I have not captured the light, I have tried, like the lens grinder, to focus the rays.

A stanza by the poet Wallace Stevens has inspired the arrangement of this book and provided the words of its title.

He never supposed
That he might be truth, himself, or part of it,
That the things that he rejected might be part
And the irregular turquoise, part, the perceptible blue
Grown denser, part, the eye so touched, so played
Upon by clouds, the ear so magnified
By thunder, parts, and all these things together,
Parts, and more things, parts. He never supposed divine
Things might not look divine, nor that if nothing
Was divine then all things were, the world itself,
And that if nothing was the truth, then all
Things were the truth, the world itself was the truth.

I interpret these lines as a kind of theophany, a visit from God or at least a glimpse of Him. In a world that does not explain itself, that mocks our desire for reduction and order, the poet perceives a veiled dimension. It is as if life's mystery were suddenly translated into a known language. Like a geode that, when tapped, opens its rough surface to reveal perfect, gleaming crystals, so here the world opens itself to expose its divine inner chamber, its holy of holies. The poet is struck by the force of his own being: the eye is touched; the ear is magnified by thunder, summoning to Jewish memory the ancient thunder at Sinai. There, too, God's presence was felt.

In this poem I see mirrored a version of my own quest: to distill from the transitory a fraction of the eternal; to discover, or perhaps to recover, those truths that hover, like atoms, beyond the scope of everyday perception. I have written here of how I see and how I am blind, of what I hear and of the sounds that escape me. I have tried to articulate those powers of spirit that I would call, in the poet's phrase, divine things.

The ancient rabbis teach that the Torah is from heaven, not in heaven. By this they mean that the divine truth is here with us. We have only to watch for it and listen for it. The Torah is the first word of God, not the last.

the eye so
touched

Not Seeing Is Believing

THERE IS A STORY of a newly ordained rabbi preparing to give his first sermon. Aware of his inexperience and hoping for his success, a committee was assembled to advise him before his debut. They asked him what he proposed to speak about.

"I thought I would speak on the weekly reading from Scripture," he told them. "It is about Abraham's encounter with God by the terebinths of Mamre."

They looked at each other uneasily. Finally one of them said: "Rabbi, couldn't you talk about something more... familiar?"

He thought for a moment. "I see what you mean," he said. "What if I talk about how God spoke to Moses from the burning bush. That would be familiar, wouldn't it?"

Again they exchanged looks. "But, Rabbi," one of them said, "what about something more... relevant, important to people's lives?"

The young rabbi pondered. "Well, he said, "what if I just talk about God, the Holy One, blessed be He. What could be more important than that?"

This time the committee groaned aloud. Seeing that he was on the wrong track, the rabbi said: "Well, then, what *should* I talk about?"

"You know," they said. "Talk about... talk about Judaism!"

This is a story that doesn't always make Jews laugh, and

perhaps it is not all that funny. There is too much truth in it. That the subject of God is antique or irrelevant has long been assumed by many of us. That it is possible to defy, deny, or simply ignore God has often been demonstrated. To speak about Judaism without mentioning God has become, in our days, not an absurdity but an art. The name of God is ceremonially confined to invocations. Acts of God refer to exclusions on insurance policies. The very word "God" has now been deleted from the English translations in some Jewish prayer books, as if it were an embarrassment.

Ancient Jews were not ashamed to believe in God. If the Hebrew Bible is an accurate reflection, they perceived God much as we perceive air: it cannot be seen, but no life is possible without it. Air is not something one "believes in"; it is not something to which one extends, or from which one withholds, intellectual assent. It is, rather, what one relies upon for every breath, what is more vital than anything visible, and what can, when it is stirred, reveal an awesome power. The ancients may have questioned God's justice, but they never doubted His dominion. The first sentence of the Torah says, "In the beginning God created...." His existence is not debated. He is already there. (I use the word "He" throughout this book as a translation from the Hebrew, not as a definition of gender.)

But we are not our ancestors. Reverence for God, once the foundation of our existence, is now the least of our concerns. God has become a concept or perhaps a superstition. Belief in God is for children. The Torah is a legend. Jewish faith today is like a dry riverbed: where once there gushed a torrent, now there is only a tiny stream. We have replaced the religion of faith with the religion of skepticism. If it can't be explained or measured, if it can't be defined or deducted, it isn't real. If I don't see it, if I can't touch it, it isn't there. We have come to conceive of truth as something that proceeds from a fact-finding survey.

What we fail to realize is that this way of thinking is just that: a way of thinking, not necessarily to be equated with wisdom. Its most obvious flaw is that it blinds us to anything that fails to identify itself as a matter of fact. We trust only the work of our own hands and the product of our own minds, and whatever lies beyond is considered an illusion.

But just because we choose to see the world that way does not make it so. I think of what it is like to walk the city streets at night, so accustomed to the glare of the neon signs and phosphor lamps that we cannot even see the sky. So entranced are we by the light of our own making that the very stars go unnoticed. But they are still there, even when we do not see them, and all of our light is only a fraction of theirs.

To speak of God, of course, is not to claim acquaintance. The medieval rabbi Joseph Albo said, "If I knew Him, I would be He." Even Moses, the prophet of prophets, was given to approach God only in thick darkness. The great philosopher Maimonides concluded that one could properly speak only of what God is not: "When tongues aspire to magnify God, all eloquence turns to ineptitude." In the phrase of Abraham Joshua Heschel, "God begins where words end."

There is another danger to speaking about God: it sounds so sanctimonious. It implies possession of a privileged insight denied to others. Belief, for anyone who has tried it, is a struggle. Even Abraham challenged God; even Sarah doubted Him; even Moses wavered. Faith can be tested and found wanting. When it encounters undeserved suffering, it often founders and probably should. Faith is not a conquered peak but a daunting ascent; not a safe harbor but a long voyage. No one hands faith to us. There are only hands to hold as we search for it together.

In the ancient days of the desert tabernacle, the holy of holies was where God's presence was thought to rest. Only the high priest could enter there, and only once a year on the Day of Atonement. Even then he was to veil himself in smoke so that he could not see. "And Aaron, the high priest, shall take from the altar a censer full of coals of fire, and he shall bring it within the holy of holies. Then he shall put incense upon the fire so that smoke covers the ark, lest he die." In this passage and throughout the Torah, God's presence is always concealed. "Thou canst not see My face," God says, "for man shall not see Me and live." On Mount Sinai there was smoke as from a furnace. In the desert there was a pillar of cloud. In the tabernacle there was a veil; within the veil there was more smoke. What is the Torah trying to tell us?

Note how the Torah's account reverses our modern perspective. For us, the question is whether there is a God. For our biblical forebears, this was not in doubt. We are afraid that we won't find God. They were afraid that they would. We insist that seeing is believing. For them, it was just the opposite. They understood that God's presence is hidden. For them, *not* seeing was believing.

At first this idea seems strange, or in modern parlance, "counter-intuitive." But it is not unlike the truth that modern astronomers have found. They estimate that more than 90 percent of the matter in the universe is invisible. In a "black hole," gravity is so powerful that not even light can escape. Even if a black hole is proven to exist, one could never see it. As in the holy of holies, so at the heart of the universe, the ultimate truth is veiled.

The writer David Bosworth, in *From My Father, Singing*, has described what he saw one day in a marsh not far from his home. It was a heron, a great wild bird, gliding over the water just a few feet above the surface. He could see the bird's long neck and the slender bulb of its skull, designed to slip through the strongest winds. The slow beat of its enormous wings, the ease of its flight, expressed the sovereignty of a creature perfectly adapted to its given world. His eyes traced its line of flight to the opposite shore, where it began to slow—its body tilting, its wings now angled—until it descended upon the branch of a fallen tree half submerged in water. There the long neck unfolded; the wings drew in against the body. Then, its roost secured, the heron froze: a slight ruffling of the tail, a minute adjustment in the angle of the head, then no motion at all. What happened next, Bosworth writes, is that the heron—disappeared. It was there. It was gone. It was there, then gone: even as he stared at it, the bird dissolved before his eyes. Within a moment of having lighted on the fallen tree, the heron had so sunk into its setting—its feathers blending with the bark, the shape of its body with the trunk of the tree—that it seemed to have vanished.

"I blinked in disbelief," Bosworth writes. "More than an uncanny act of camouflage, the bird—so huge, so compelling only seconds before—actually seemed to have disappeared. It required an act of concentration bordering on faith, depending as much on memory as on sense, to extract a heron from the visual array of trees, water and sand, to find the living bird. To me, dumb witness on the beach, the abrupt transition from bird to branch, from perfect motion to perfect stillness, seemed more awesome than the bird in flight. It was there. It was gone. It merged, this majestic bird, it submerged within its world, before my eyes."

Upon reading this, I thought of the God of Israel veiled in smoke and cloud. I thought of the idea that *not* seeing is believing. Is it not possible that what is true of the heron is also true of God, that His presence is hidden before our eyes, here and yet not here, disguised by its perfect fit?

Bosworth's epiphany was to glimpse the invisible, to behold the hidden order that routinely escapes us. We are more readily inclined to narrow our vision to the task at hand. The brain tends to reduce reality to the forms we recognize. Gestalt theory calls this *Pragnanz,* the idea that the visual system converges on the most regular perception conceived by the senses. It is a necessary compression of reality; human consciousness is rarely capable of more.

The rabbis teach that when divine truth was revealed to the biblical prophets, it was as if the world were suffused by a momentary flash of lightning. But for Moses, who beheld God "face to face," it was as if the lightning never ceased. Ordinary mortals cannot bear such vivid clarity. To see the heron everywhere is beyond our powers. That may explain why, for so many of us, it is also beyond our belief.

What we know most intimately, we cease to notice. A fish would be the last to recognize water. One wonders whether a snow leopard or a sandpiper ever sees the element for which it is named. It is certainly true of our own tacit apprehensions. Psychologists call them "visual invariants": the things we see without noticing or recognize without acknowledging. They might include the stop sign at the corner, the tree in the yard, the car keys or the toothbrush. They might include the stars in the sky. At our most oblivious, they might even include a wife or a husband or a child. Yet if we fail to see these images of God before our eyes, how will we ever see Him?

"The God who sees is never seen," says the Talmud. Yet it is the conviction of Judaism that He is there, and here. He is not unknowable; He is unnoticed. "Moses looked," says the Torah, "and behold, the bush was all aflame, yet the bush was not consumed. And Moses said: 'I will turn aside now and see this great sight, that the bush is not burned.' And when the Lord saw that he turned aside to see, God called to him from the midst of the bush." The words are familiar. But notice this: God does not call until Moses turns to look. According to the rabbis, others had passed this bush before; only Moses noticed it.

"God is not always silent," Heschel has written, "and man is not always blind. In every life there are moments when there is a lifting of the veil at the horizon of the known." It might be the sight of a bird that disappears before our eyes. It might be the first trace of dawn on the rim of night. It might be a moment of tenderness. It might be that, like the heron on the pond, God is disguised in the ordinary, submerged in what surrounds us. The potential for recognition lies within. If we can be awake to beauty, alert to wonder, alive to love, then there will be moments when we behold His glory.

EVIDENCE OF GOD

IN THE SEVENTH GRADE I was taught by an elderly English teacher named Mrs. Plummer. We all thought that Mrs. Plummer, aside from being ancient, was also a bit eccentric. Every day she would bring something unremarkable to class: a leaf, a feather, a dandelion, a seashell. We thought we were much too old for this kind of thing; "show and tell" was for kindergarten. But Mrs. Plummer wanted us to look at these objects, to *see* them. She always talked about "the beauty of the commonplace." In her quavery voice she would recite the stanza by William Blake:

> To see a world in a grain of sand
> And a Heaven in a wild flower,
> Hold infinity in the palm of your hand
> And Eternity in an hour.

We couldn't help but like Mrs. Plummer, but we weren't always sure that we knew—or that she knew—what she was talking about. And more's the pity.

There is a verse in the book of Genesis that Mrs. Plummer would have appreciated. The patriarch Jacob falls asleep and dreams of a ladder stretching from earth to heaven, upon which angels are ascending and descending. When he awakens, Jacob exclaims, "Surely the Lord is present in this place, and I did not know it!" Or as one commentator, Samson Raphael Hirsch, has expressed it: "So God is *here!* So one need not go to heaven to look for God; He is *here!* And until now I did not know it! Until now my eyes were closed...."

A Hasidic tradition takes Jacob's insight even further. God created the visible world, one rebbe has taught, as a way of describing Himself. The creation we see is a kind of parable by which God may be understood. It is a divine language, a visual grammar. A glimpse of God does not require a vision of angels, but merely, as the poet said, a grain of sand.

Heschel often dwelled on this point. We tend to think of God, he writes, as if we were here and He were there; as if, in the Torah's phrase, we must journey across the oceans or beyond the stars to find Him. But if we fail, it is not because we do not know how to look far enough. It is because we do not know how to look *near* enough. "Surely God is in this place, and I did not know it!" Most of the time, we don't.

In a local newspaper there used to be a daily column called "The Question Man." Once the question was: "Why don't you believe in God?" While the negative wording may have called for a certain kind of response, many would agree with the replies. A social worker named Susan said: "I don't believe or not believe. There's no real reason to believe. No one's ever shown me anything so I should believe." A railway clerk named Marlene agreed: "There's no reason to believe. I see no evidence of God." Susan and Marlene, like many of us, want evidence. If we can't prove it, it isn't true. If we can't touch it, it isn't real. If we can't see it, it isn't there. We see no evidence of God. But would we know Him if we saw Him?

In one of her essays, Cynthia Ozick describes how we tend to divide everyday experience into two categories: the usual and the unusual; the commonplace and the remarkable; the ordinary and the extraordinary. When something extraordinary is happening, we are bound to know it: the high, terrifying, tragic, and ecstatic moments are unmistakable in any life. They insist on being noticed. When Jacob beheld the flight of angels, it was hardly something he could ignore.

The extraordinary does not let you shrug your shoulders and walk away.

But the ordinary is not like that. Because it accompanies us all the time, the ordinary does not insist on being noticed. It is so evident, so obvious, that it disappears. The ordinary doesn't frighten or enrapture. All it does is grant us life. It brings us the safe return of the school bus. It provides one meal after another, puts one foot in front of the other. It lets us take for granted the very things that most deserve our gratitude, from the air we breathe to the pulse in our veins, from the light of the sun to the touch of a loving hand.

What Jacob discovered, and what Mrs. Plummer was trying to teach us, is a profound truth: nothing is ordinary. The ordinary is only the extraordinary in the guise of the familiar. That the sun rises every morning may make each sunrise less surprising, but no less glorious. A bundle of roses may make each blossom less conspicuous, but no less lovely. There *is* beauty in the commonplace; everywhere we look, there is evidence of God. Divine things are often disguised as ordinary things.

The function of art, Victor Shklovsky has observed, is to "defamiliarize" the familiar, to make the world strange. An artist is one who can overcome the deadening effects of habit upon human perception. Habit devours objects; art recovers them. Art restores the sensation of life, the miracle of being. What Shklovsky defines as art, Jacob describes as faith.

Mere sight is what we see; insight is how we see it. Mere sight can only behold; it takes insight to comprehend. Both the eyes and the heart must be open. The essence of religion is to see God in the commonplace, to see the extraordinary in the ordinary. In the Talmud it is said that a Jew should recite no less than one hundred blessings every day. There is a Hebrew blessing for practically every sight and sound, every fragrance, every morsel of food, every dusk and every dawn. There is a blessing upon hearing thunder or seeing lightning.

There is a blessing for the sight of the sea and the mountains, for a new moon or a new blossom. All of these are with us every day, and for that very reason we tend to overlook them. But the rabbis insist that to live so insensibly is to commit a theft against God, impoverishing His creation and robbing our own lives of their deepest joy. It is when we realize that all of life is a divine gift that we discover the truth of Jacob's insight: "So this is where God is, right here in this very place!"

Across all the years I can still hear Mrs. Plummer reciting one of her favorite poems in her quavery voice:

> Dear Lord, I know You care for me
> How very many times I see
> The signs You leave throughout the day
> To let me know You passed this way.
> How could I ever disbelieve
> Who feel Your hand upon my sleeve?
> Nor lose my way throughout the land
> Who find Your footprints in the sand?
> And though my mind is much too small
> To weigh the wonder of it all
> I know that You are every place,
> I do not have to see Your face.

There is also a Hebrew blessing to be recited upon beholding a person of great wisdom. If Mrs. Plummer were still here, I would say one for her.

Technology

Occasionally in the Hebrew Bible one encounters rituals that have vanished from civilization. The descriptions of these rituals cannot always be understood; even when scholars try, their theories are confined to speculation.

For instance, among the vestments of the high priest was a kind of ornamental shield worn over the heart. Inside this shield were placed objects called urim and thummim. Scholars think that these were ritual devices to detect the will of God. Writing in the first century, the historian Josephus describes them as light-emitting gems. His contemporary Philo of Alexandria pictures them as embroidered images like the oracle symbols of Egypt. At least one modern scholar has suggested that the urim and thummim were little coded stones, something like dice.

Or consider the ritual of the red cow. Biblical law prescribes a process of purification for a person who has touched a corpse. The purification is accomplished by slaughtering an unblemished red cow, incinerating it, mixing its ashes with water, and sprinkling the solution over the person's body. After undergoing this ritual twice in a seven-day period, the person washes his clothes, bathes, and is thus cleansed of the contamination of the corpse. That even the ancients were baffled by this procedure is reflected in rabbinic writings. According to the Mishnah, the ritual was rarely performed; according to the Midrash, even the wisest of men, King Solomon, could not explain it. Modern scholars have suggested that contact with a corpse was thought to convey both physical and spiritual pollution that could be cleansed only by extraordinary efforts. Still others have seen the red cow as a symbolic expiation for the golden calf worshiped by the Israelites at Sinai.

In truth, as in the case of the urim and thummim, the red cow is a mystery to us. But we do not need to know exactly what these rituals meant in order to understand what they represent. They were the applied science of the age, the attempt to master the unknown or unintelligible. As we use radar antennas and microprocessors, so our ancestors used the technology of their invention, whether amulets or oracles or the ashes of a red cow. Of course, we tend to think of technology as a phenomenon peculiar to our own times. But before we dismiss the backward theories of our forebears, we might do well to see our science in the light of theirs.

We have much to be proud of: antibiotics, integrated circuits, frozen food. We have measured the stars and walked the moon. We have transplanted the heart and split the atom. We have invented machines that think faster than we can. In the flush of such accomplishment, it is not surprising that we regard our ancient predecessors with a certain condescension.

Yet compared to even the most prosaic designs of nature, we too are technological primitives. No engineer has yet been able to fuse the delicacy and simplicity of a butterfly wing. No shipbuilder has been able to duplicate the streamlined contour of a blue shark. No motor can compare to the silent, efficient power of our own muscles. No camera can match the miniature perfection of our own eyes. "The narrowest hinge in my hand," wrote Walt Whitman, "puts to scorn all machinery."

It is not only the poet who sees the gulf between our powers of invention and nature's. There is a modern science called biomechanics whose purpose is to discern the technology of life as we find it. These scientists have studied, for example, the fluid mechanics of an ordinary fish. The more they learn, the more perfection they find. The mouth of the fish is at the point of highest pressure, allowing water to enter. The gill covers are located at the point of lowest pressure, allowing it to escape. Where the pressure is positive, that is, inward, its bony skull prevents the fish from collapsing. Where the pressure is outward and negative, there is a tension-resistant skin. The eyes of the fish are located exactly at the point where pressure goes from positive to negative, assuring that the focus of the eyes will not change with swimming velocity. From a technological perspective, the fish is perfectly designed to make pressure distribution work for it rather than against it. As the poet said of the human hand, so also the humblest fish "puts to scorn all machinery."

Perhaps the loss of religious sensibility in our day may be attributed in part to the loss of the poet's perspective. Our generation likes to think that it is more intelligent and more capable than all the others. But every generation entertains the same conceit. We look back upon the amulets and the ashes as primitive relics. But the computers and calculators of today are the urim and thummim of tomorrow. No matter what we do, it will never compare to what a power beyond ours has already done. No matter what we ever know, it will only be a fraction of what we will never know.

This truth is not far to seek. It confronts us at every turn, in ways large and small. Some time ago I read a modest observation written by a man who lived near a pond. One day he noticed that a pair of geese had begun nesting on a small island out in the middle of the water. A heavy rain fell for several days. Afterward the man looked for the geese again. At first he could not find them. The island at the center of the pond had all but disappeared beneath the rising waters. But then he saw a little mound of earth, just large enough for the two geese. It was all that was left of the island. The male stood beside his nesting mate, watching the waters recede.

How was it, the man wondered, that the geese had unerringly chosen the highest, safest ground for their nest? We might call it instinct. But what is instinct if not the divine technology, that which we cannot understand, at which we can only marvel?

The red cow and the urim and thummim were part of the ancient attempt to confront the unknown. Modern science may be an advance, but ultimately it too is only a surmise. The greatest scientist of his age, Isaac Newton, came to the same conclusion. "We are like children," he wrote, "playing with pebbles on the seashore, while the great ocean of truth rolls, unexplored, beyond our reach."

Shining objects

SOME TIME AGO there was a burglary of a local synagogue. What the thieves wanted were the silver crowns and breastplates that adorn the Torah scrolls. Nothing else was missing. The scrolls were left alone.

At the time I remember feeling almost grateful that the intruders refrained from vandalizing the scrolls or desecrating them. But then it dawned on me that the scrolls were undamaged not out of respect but out of indifference. To the thieves the silver was valuable, the scrolls worthless. The Torahs were discarded like so much debris, like the wrapping paper we tear away to get at the object we really want.

Yet it is the scrolls, more than the silver, that are cherished by Jewish belief. In the ancient words of the book of Proverbs, the Torah's value is "greater than silver or fine gold; it is more precious than rubies; no treasure can match it." Obviously the thieves did not agree with the biblical appraisal, and it is safe to say that they are not alone.

We live in the midst of a culture gripped by a terrible thirst for material things. It is a culture that calls people "consumers," where the "standard of living" refers to material comfort, as if there is no other standard worth measuring. It is a culture that reduces life to the accumulation of possessions and relentless contests for prestige, that reveres what the hands can hold and sneers at the intangible. It is a culture, in short, that prefers the silver to the scrolls.

But what becomes of those who fall under the spell of the

silver? The Yiddish playwright S. Ansky tells a story about such a person, a man rich in possessions but impoverished in spirit. Somehow he is persuaded to pay a visit to the rebbe. The rebbe leads him to the window. "Look out there," the rebbe says, and the rich man looks out at the street. "What do you see?"

"I see people," answers the rich man.

Again the rebbe takes his hand, and this time he leads him to the mirror. "What do you see now?"

The rich man answers, "Now I see myself."

"So," the rebbe says. "In the window there is glass and in the mirror there is glass. But the glass of the mirror is covered with a little silver, and no sooner is the silver added than you cease to see others but see only yourself."

That is what can happen to us under the spell of our possessions. They are all we see. At first we possess them; before long they possess us. They confine our ambition to the satisfaction of our desires. We become so obsessed with what we have that we fail to realize what we have become.

A parable is related by the ancient rabbis. It is about a fox who lusted after the sweet grapes of a vineyard on the other side of a high stone wall. There was a tiny opening in the wall, and the fox had to fast for three days before he was thin enough to squeeze through. Inside he gorged himself on the sweet grapes, but then he became so fat that he couldn't get out. So again he had to fast and fast until he was thin enough to squeeze through the opening again. When the fox finally got out, he pondered the matter: "What good are all the riches of the vineyard when you have to be thin to get in and thin to get out?" It is true: we leave this world the same way we came in, in the same frail house of clay that is our body, with only the soul still trembling inside.

If we could spend our days searching for truth instead of advantage, we would probably spend them differently. But only vigilant eyes can find the truth amid all that is glaring and superficial. Astronomers speak of "naked-eye objects," the comets and meteors that streak through the sky in bright showers of light. They dazzle and impress. Yet by their very flamboyance, they also obscure. Less visible to the naked eye is a far greater inventory of wonder. A distant star is not as conspicuous as a comet, but its light is of a far greater magnitude, and it abides beyond the moment. The naked eye will never see the gravity that holds the stars in thrall. Nor will it see the mantle of air that ignites a naked-eye object in the first place. As in the heavens, so in the orbit of our own lives: the eye is captivated by shining objects.

When I was a child, I eagerly awaited the Hanukkah festival. That is when my grandmother would bring to my sisters and me chocolate coins wrapped in bright gold foil: Hanukkah gelt, we called it. I remember how we watched like hawks for her hand to emerge from her purse with the little gilt bags of treasure. In those years my head scarcely reached my grandmother's waist, and I don't think I even looked at her face when she brought the candy. My eyes were on the shiny Hanukkah gelt, more precious to me then than the loving gaze and embrace that came with it.

"Why," asks the prophet Isaiah, "do you spend money for what is not bread?" How truly he spoke! How often we consider the worthless to be precious, and the precious to be worthless. What I would give now, how much Hanukkah gelt I would spend, for just one gaze from my grandmother, one of her embraces, a fleeting touch of her hand. For now I can have Hanukkah gelt whenever I want, but she is gone forever.

I think of the terse poem of Samuel Menashe:

> My mother once said to me
> "When one sees the tree in leaf,
> One thinks the beauty of the tree is in its leaves.
> And then one sees the bare tree."

PERSISTENCE OF VISION

ONCE WHEN I WAS AT A MOVIE THEATER, a projector malfunctioned. For a moment the image on the screen blurred. Then it began to flutter, at first almost imperceptibly, like a hummingbird; then more slowly, until one could see individual frames in rapid succession. Finally the operator stopped the film, and the screen went dark.

Although I had been dimly aware of the technology of the motion picture, seeing it revealed so graphically came as something of a surprise. A motion picture is a sequence of still pictures moving very fast. Each picture is flashed on the screen for a fraction of a second, followed by another in which the position of the subject is slightly altered. But if the pictures were projected continuously rather than separately, the image would blur. To prevent this, the shutter revolves between frames, alternating flashes of light with darkness. The screen is actually dark for a longer period of time than it is lit. What, then, accounts for the verisimilitude of motion? Why don't we notice the darkness?

The answer lies in a property of the eye called "persistence of vision." When the eye sees an object under a bright light, the visual image persists momentarily in darkness. Each frame on the motion picture screen appears before the last one has faded from visual memory. The ability of the eye to retain an image while beholding another image creates the impression of continuous movement. The viewer's persistence of vision subtracts the intervals of darkness.

It occurs to me that persistence of vision is a phenomenon that transcends the physiology of the eye. It describes a way of thinking no less than a way of seeing: the ability to keep intact a mental image, to visualize light in darkness. It is a spiritual condition, registering hope as the eye registers light.

The writer Frank Conroy has recounted a story recalled from his youth in New York City. At age sixteen he worked selling hot dogs at a stand in a subway station, one level above the trains and one level below the street. It was a dreary place to work and dreary work to do. Down the corridor from him was a shoeshine stand attended by two men. On his break he would often pass the time with them. They were never very busy: their stand was located in a dark corner, half hidden by columns. He would sit with them and watch while they moved around the elevated chairs and the shelves of rags and shoe polish.

Here is the unusual thing he noticed about the two men: they were always staring into the distance. Talking, working, smoking, waiting: their eyes were always somewhere else. It could not have been the corridor that attracted their notice; there was nothing there to see. Watching the two men as the weeks went by, he realized that they never looked at anything in their immediate vicinity. They did not even look at their customers, except for the instant that it took to discern the color of their shoes. Even then they rarely looked at what they were doing, but rubbed in the polish, brushed and buffed the shoes by feel, all the while looking over their shoulders into the distance, as if awaiting some arrival.

Only years later, Conroy writes, long after he had left the subway for a better job, did he reflect upon the two shoeshine men and their long, steady staring off into space. There they were, in a dark corner of a subway station, bent over people's feet. Their staring off, he suggests, was an assertion of autonomy, a ritual of freedom, a persistence of vision. In the darkness of the subway, their eyes still registered light. The image of hope within was held intact. My body is here, their eyes said, but that is all. My soul is somewhere else, far away from here, above the ground where the light is. The back that is bent over your shoes belongs to a person who stands up straight. Just because you are up there in that chair, and I am down here at your feet, does not mean that I am any less than you.

Persistence of vision is more ancient than Conroy's recollection. The biblical Hebrews, too, were consigned to shadows and dark corners. They, too, had to subsist on the barest of margins. They, too, were bent over the feet of the taskmaster. They knew the despair of living this way. But like the shoeshine men, they knew something else: that the soul cannot be trapped underground. The Hebrew slaves, too, lifted their eyes, stared into the distance, and dreamed of deliverance. They too insisted upon their irreducible divine dignity, regardless of their lowly station.

Their journey to freedom was not theirs alone. Nor is it confined to one people or to one place. It is the journey of every soul, of every vision that persists in darkness. As God spoke from the mountain, so He speaks in the subway; as His voice called from a thornbush, so it calls from a shoeshine stand. The message has not changed in three thousand years: the worth of a person is bestowed by God, and by God alone. It is His flame that burns within us, His light that persists, that none can diminish, that none can extinguish.

Angels

WHEN THE EXPEDITION OF MAGELLAN reached the shores of Tierra del Fuego, it is said that the natives barely noticed. It was not that they were accustomed to visitors; their land was as remote as any on earth. It was, in fact, just the opposite: so strange was the sight of great ships in the harbor that they could not decode the visual evidence. There was nothing in their experience of reality to register these seafaring apparitions, so unlike the canoes of their ancestral usage. The limits of human vision are not determined by the retina alone. They have to do also with the scope of imagination. What we cannot comprehend, we are not likely to notice. What we cannot imagine, we are not likely to see.

I am thinking about angels. We moderns have heard of them. We have read about their encounters with our biblical ancestors. But we have never seen an angel, at least not to our knowledge. Having measured the heavens with spectrographs, having reduced the universe to numerical equations, we no longer traffic with angels. Equipped to recognize heavenly bodies, we no longer acknowledge heavenly beings.

Angelology was once a fairly elaborate branch of knowledge. The legions of heaven included archangels, ministering angels, guardian angels, and alas, fallen ones. Aside from the cherubim and seraphim mentioned in the Hebrew Bible, later Jewish literature also attests to angels of power and angels of dominion, angels of light and angels of darkness. According to the medieval *ofanim*, Hebrew liturgical poems depicting visions of heaven, angels are creatures of flame, half fire and half water; they are the color of pearl and turquoise; they are as strong as palm trees and as numerous as locusts. Their beating wings are like the sound of rushing waters echoing through the heavens, exclaiming the glory of God.

Two thousand years ago, in the era of apocalyptic visions, it occasionally happened that someone was transported to the upper world for a glimpse of the angels at work. He would return and report what he saw. We can still read these dispatches in the Apocrypha and Pseudepigrapha that have survived. Angels were visible at the four corners of the throne of glory. They were singing divine serenades, watching over the house of Israel, and moving freely through the palace of God. If you were in heaven, you couldn't miss them.

But here on earth . . . that is another matter. Or so the rabbis thought. When the angels leave heaven, whether to convey a divine message or to intercede in human affairs, they assume a disguise. Sometimes they will appear as ordinary people, at other times in other forms. According to the Talmud, they can stand and sit, speak and walk. They can wear clothes and ride horses. Because they are sent by God but look for all the world like us, these messenger angels are often the source of confusion.

Consider, for example, one of the first biblical encounters, recorded in the book of Genesis. "The Lord appeared to Abraham by the terebinths of Mamre. He looked up and saw three men." Already there is a problem: how can God, who cannot be seen, appear as a man? Even if He did, why three men? The noted rabbinic commentator Rashbam suggests that the mention of God's name in the first sentence is a giveaway that the three are really angels. An even greater authority, Rashi, explains that Abraham was so accustomed to visits from angels that he simply thought of them as men. The Torah continues to call them men until the next chapter of Genesis, when they are finally called angels, except now there are two of them.

Angels are tricky. Perhaps the most famous case befell Abraham's grandson, Jacob. Alone one night on a riverbank, he is set upon by an unnamed man who will not give Jacob his name. The Torah does not give it either. But the rabbis were sure that he was an angel.

Among the ancients, the self was conceived as a hierarchy of spirit extending from the sensible to the celestial world. A chain of intermediaries connected them to God. Like many of the convictions that our ancestors cherished, this one has since been consigned to the realm of myth. A belief in angels is not exactly respectable today, since it suggests a less sophisticated and less immaculate form of monotheism.

But that is not our real problem with angels. Before we can believe that God sends us messengers, we have to believe that God sends us anything. Before we can imagine what heaven is like, we have to imagine that heaven exists. So accustomed are we to the sight of the empty harbor that we cannot imagine a ship. We probably wouldn't know one if we saw one.

"Angels change their names," Rashi says. What if he was right? What if one can't tell for sure who they are or where they are lurking? What if we are seeing angels all the time? What if they are all around us, very close to us, as close as those we love?

The dance of atoms, writes Christopher Leach, is as awesome as the flight of angels. We need not revert to ancient belief for a sense of the miraculous or a glimpse of the sublime. Yet I cannot help but think that something is lost in the translation from angels to atoms. It is as if we dwelled on the shores of Tierra del Fuego, oblivious to the ships in the harbor, ships we cannot see.

The lens

O URS IS A CULTURE obsessed with the immediate. Because we tend to measure the importance of events by how recently they happened, the trivial replaces the signal. The present is the focus, the fashion of the moment. On television, radio, and webcast, the news is updated by the hour, even by the minute. The announcer's two-word segue—"Now this . . . "—is the litany of our times.

Living in the age of high technology, at the heart of the information revolution where even last week is obsolete, the past is something archaic, a dead letter. After all, once you have invented the adding machine, the abacus is discarded; and once you have invented the computer, the adding machine in its turn becomes a relic.

But human generations are not like generations of machines. Human beings need to look backward in order to understand what they are and what they may yet become. Otherwise we lose our way. Albert Einstein once described our plight as the perfection of means but the confusion of ends. More and more we moderns know how to do things but not why. We can clone new animals and copyright them, but without the conviction of a higher purpose than profit. In our preoccupation with new facts, we lose touch with old truths.

As Mary Hesse has observed, modern science inclines to a certain conceit, the notion of a royal and single road to knowledge. Science aspires to a kind of imperialism that claims exclusive access to the essences and true causes of the world, which it claims to express in exact language amenable to logic. But Hesse, herself a scientist, points out that scientific method is only one of the ways to make sense of the world. It is comparable, not necessarily superior, to other models, metaphors, and myths. Science answers to our practical purposes with regard to nature. But as Einstein suggests, procedure is not purpose; method is not meaning.

Judaism is not a very scientific idea, nor is it a modern one. It is rarely in tune with prevailing fashions. Unlike the daily news, it offers no consumer price index or Dow Jones average, no exact measurement of success or performance. Judaism is not about how much, but about what for; not about technique, but purpose. The divine commandments do not reach the tabloids. The headlines there may be remembered for a day or even for a week, but the Scriptures have been remembered for millennia, because they speak to the depths of the human experience. Religion is not about how to make a living but how to make a life. That is a challenge we have in common with our ancestors, and that is why the ancient wisdom still matters.

Recently I came across the account of a helicopter pilot who flew from an aircraft carrier far out at sea. "I was flying the helicopter back to the ship," he wrote, "when a heavy fog rolled in. I couldn't see a thing. Flying at a low altitude, I knew that a single mistake would plunge us into the ocean. Worse yet, I was experiencing a complete loss of balance, which is common for pilots flying without visual guidance. The vertigo was so bad that despite the instrument readings I was convinced that I was lying on my side. For fifteen minutes I flew the helicopter by its instruments, as I had been taught, fighting the urge to turn it. When we finally broke safely through the fog, I saw that my training had not been for nothing. I was thankful that I had relied on the instruments rather than on my impulse."

For a believing Jew, the divine commandments are the instruments, and the Torah of Moses is the compass. No matter what the fashion, no matter how prevalent the culture of the moment, the ancient ideals are the steady stars that steer the course of faith. For the contemporary mind to escape the tyranny of the present, the first task is to regard the past without condescension. Through all that is alien and archaic, we must learn to permit voyage, to be guided by the worn but still durable instruments of measure.

Some two centuries ago, the French thinker Condorcet described human history as an inevitable progress toward perfection. Given what has happened since then—Auschwitz comes to mind—such confidence would seem unwarranted. Yet we persist in believing that we are the climax of all human effort, that we know more about everything than everyone else who ever lived, that the past was a darkness from which we have finally emerged. We inhabit the present as if the long voyage leading up to it was merely a rehearsal for our debut. Our moment in time looms larger than all the rest.

In contrast, it may be of benefit to consider the verdict of Judaism. In rabbinic tradition, the spiritual insight of the Torah is revered above our own. The Torah is regarded as a closer approximation of the divine truth than anything of which we are capable. Certainly the Torah's lens of vision is different from ours. Often when we moderns look through it, everything seems to be out of focus. We assume that there is something wrong with the lens. It never occurs to us that there might be something wrong with our eyes.

Dandelions

A WEED IS A PLANT that grows where it isn't wanted. Its two basic characteristics are unruliness and profusion. Weeds show up uninvited, and they grow in multitudes. Take, by way of example, the dandelion. Here is a weed if ever there was one. Dandelions love to sprout on manicured lawns, where they are unwelcome; and you never see just one of them. They are among the most prolific of weeds, shooting up here, there, and everywhere, without evident design or purpose.

But there is a new theory about the dandelion and other weeds like it. This theory holds that our eyes deceive us, as eyes often do. We confuse the "individual" dandelion that we see with the whole dandelion beneath the earth. According to evolutionary biology, we are mistaking, so to speak, the finger for the hand. The dandelion is not merely a little stem with a fuzzy head; it is actually a very large tree—without a trunk, without major branches, without permanent roots—but a kind of tree nonetheless. Hardly a random assortment of useless vegetation, it is an evolutionary individual (EI), recognized as a distinct creature by its genetic oneness rather than by its physical boundaries. What appears to the eye to be disconnected and chaotic, a mere tangle of weeds, is profoundly connected and unified, a single organism.

What strikes me about this theory is its potential to explain more than dandelions. Think of the human race. Think of all the unwelcome lives, often regarded with hostility, often showing up where they are not wanted, growing too profusely to be valued. Think of those assorted lives, visibly separate, disconnected, like dandelions in the field. Then think of this: what if we, the human family, are just like the dandelion— not a jumble of weeds but fingers of the same invisible hand, blossoms of the same invisible tree, disguised by our diversity but truly one and the same being? Would this not help us to understand that we are all bound in living communion, in interwoven attachment; that there is no pain or joy or fear felt by any one of us that is not felt by all of us? As gravity binds galaxies, as electromagnetism binds molecules, is it not possible that we too are united beneath appearances? In the words of E. B. de Vito,

> I am like you. You are like me:
> We always find ourselves in others....
> It is never too far to find our brothers.
> There is nowhere to go but home.

In Ravenna are the most stunning mosaics in the world. Centuries before the Pointillists, the Ravenna masters knew that fragments of pure color, seen at the proper distance, can coalesce into images of startling depth and beauty. But the secret of the Ravenna school was to grasp how disparate shards of glass disguise an unbroken whole; how wildly assorted chips and slivers conceal a seamless fit. By setting the tesserae at slight angles to one another, the Ravenna masters found that the effect of depth is enriched, the reflections of light multiplied. The unevenness, so obvious to the eye up close, disappears at a distance. The colors emerge in unearthly splendor. In isolation, no fragment is remarkable. Only in aggregate, in ensemble, is its glory beheld.

When the Hebrew prophet Zechariah imagined the climax of time, he envisioned a final unity on earth and in heaven: "On that day the Lord shall be one, and His name one." For despite the appearance of disparity, we are all of us bound together in one design. Beyond the boundaries that appear to divide us is a divine gravity that holds us fast.

If only we could see like the masters of Ravenna; if only we could learn what the dandelion knows.

The binary eye

L ITERAL INTERPRETATION has never been the practice of the Jewish sages. For them, each word and each letter of the Torah is divinely encoded and susceptible of any number of meanings. To probe no further than the surface of the text would be like studying the Torah scroll without unrolling it. Nor would the sages accept the view that the advent of science renders the ancient words obsolete. Take, for example, the Torah's description of creation. In the rabbinic view, this account does not contradict science any more than poetry contradicts prose. Both are versions of truth. We modern readers are so intent on subjecting the text to the scrutiny of science that we ignore any other way of understanding it.

In his book *And our faces, my heart, brief as photos,* John Berger has described how even a subtle shift of perspective can open unsuspected portals of vision. "On the window ledge," he writes, "hangs a shaving mirror. I see reflected in it a sprig of lilac branch: each petal of each tiny flower is vivid, distinct, near, so near that the petals look like pores of skin. At first I do not understand why what I see in the mirror is so much more intense than the rest of the branch which, in fact, is nearer to me. Then I realize that what I am looking at in the mirror is the far side of the lilac, the side fully lit by the last light of the sun." Painters, Berger explains, often seek a similar experience. When their work has reached a certain stage, they will study it in a mirror. What they see are the images reversed, transformed. The altered perspective allows them to see the painting all over again, with new eyes.

Like a painting, the Hebrew Scriptures too benefit from new angles of vision. The biblical account of creation, so often forced into Procrustean beds of doctrine, may be read more creatively: as neither myth nor fact but rather as a response to the mystery of origins; not as an eyewitness testimony to the creation but as an attempt to understand our place in it. It need not compete with scientific postulates. Rather it seeks to discern, in the vast activity of the visible world, a kind of order, sense, and purpose.

It is not unlike the theoretical physics that seeks to describe the structure of the universe and the forces that bind it together. Physicists have tried, for instance, to relate the particles of the atom to the distribution of galaxies in space. Where the atom was once seen in simple terms—proton, neutron, electron—it is now seen as a blur, a bewildering array of subatomic particles called quarks and squarks, gravitons and gluons. Physicists define their task as an effort to make sense of it all, to detect hidden symmetries, to find order in chaos.

Thousands of years separate the physicist from the biblical writer, but they share the same ambition. The ancient Hebrew tongue, while nothing like the language of mathematics, has its own precision. As biblical scholars have noted, the creation narrative is carefully modulated by the alternation of divine and human speech, description and prescription. The formality of its sequences and the repetition of key words evokes a sense of order and harmony. The first three days present the creation in its generalities—light and water, heaven and earth—and the second three present the lower order over which human beings preside. Thus there is a symmetry of functions between God and humankind. The Sabbath is the conclusion and culmination of creation, where the coordinate of space meets the coordinate of time.

Such interpretations appeal to me because of their regard

for the ancient text and its aesthetic design. Yet even this approach does not begin to tap the Torah's roots. These lie in another realm entirely.

Some time ago I was in New York City and had the chance to visit the Museum of Modern Art. There I saw the painting by Vincent Van Gogh called "The Starry Night." Presumably a landscape of a little town beneath a night sky, this painting looks nothing like what the eyes behold. The sky is rendered as a turbulent swirl of colors, like a storm-tossed ocean. The stars are as near as moons and as bright as suns. The night does not appear that way to the naked eye. But we respond to Van Gogh because he seems to see beyond the horizon. A painting is not a photograph. The artist is not a camera. In the same way, Torah is not science. Scripture is not physics. Each has its own truth, and both deserve our respect.

The ancient Greeks believed that the eye had a binary function: to collect light and to disperse it. A ray went forth from the eye and returned again with its data, like a traveler bearing gifts. Even if the Greek model has been superseded, it evinces a profound truth: our vision is determined from within and from without. Vision is not only the product of what is visible, but what is perceived, what is felt, what is believed.

If we open the Scriptures expecting to find the literal truth, the exact language of God, we delude ourselves. To study the Bible is both to discover and to search, to collect light and to disperse it. It flourishes from the infusion of altered perspectives and exposures. For the Jewish student of Torah, the search is for neither the literal nor the empirical. The search is for the eternal, for the truth beyond science or sanctimony. The search is for the countenance of God. The ancient sages were humbler than we are. They never claimed to possess the Torah's certain truth or to surpass its wisdom. "The first man did not know it perfectly," taught Ben Sirach, "nor will the last man comprehend it. For its wisdom is wider than the sea, and its counsel lies beyond the deep."

FRACTALS

O F THE FIVE BOOKS of the Pentateuch, the fourth is perhaps the least appreciated. To scholars, the book is
puzzling; to students, it is tedious. Its English title is "Numbers," referring to the census of Israel reported at the book's
outset and again toward its close. Numbers includes narrative, poetry, prophecy, prayer, oracle, census, and archive. To
the unversed reader, it is a confusing tangle of unrelated, inco-
herent data. If the origin of the Torah is claimed to be divine,
should this not be reflected by its design? Would God, wishing
to reveal His will, be so disorganized?

For the ancient rabbis, of course, this was not a possibility.
God could never be less than perfect; only our comprehension is lacking. Even in the apparent jumble of the book of
Numbers, there must be a design, if only we can detect it; and
the rabbis tried. They note, for instance, the geographical co-
hesion of the narrative, from Mount Sinai to the borders of
Canaan. The forty years in the desert comprise exactly forty
stations, which can be divided into three stages, each of which
occupies an equal proportion of the book as a whole. Once
we see it this way, a measure of its hidden structure emerges.

There are other clues. It has been shown, for example,
that while Numbers appears to switch back and forth at random between the history of Israel and the commandments
of God, there is actually a regular alternation between the
two throughout, meant perhaps to express the continuing
encounter between the mortal and the divine. A concealed

pattern is evident in smaller details too. As Jacob Milgrom has demonstrated, virtually every chapter of the book is informed by a literary pattern known as chiasm, the inversion of order in parallel phrases. This is like a poem with a hidden rhyming scheme. If you read it quickly or superficially, you may not even notice that it rhymes. So also the book of Numbers. Its design is not readily evident. Its architecture is hidden beneath the surface.

This insight from the Torah is not confined to the Torah. In 1975 a mathematician named Mandelbrot introduced the term "fractal" to describe a new way of looking at objects. Technically, fractals are a language of geometry. But unlike the Euclidean geometry learned in school—points, lines, angles—fractals are expressed as algorithms, sets of mathematical procedures. With the help of a computer, these can be translated into geometric forms unlike any we are accustomed to seeing. What they reveal, beneath the circles, triangles, and squares we routinely recognize, is a more comprehensive geometric pattern, an underlying regularity imperceptible to the eyes. For example, a river, a cloud, or a human artery do not seem to have a regular geometric shape: they are neither rectangular, oval nor round. Yet fractal geometry describes them in a new dimension. Even the most complex and intricate shapes in nature exhibit fractal architecture. "Scientists will be surprised and delighted," Mandelbrot wrote, "to find that shapes once called strange or tangled can actually be measured and quantified."

One of the most startling discoveries yielded by fractals is that many objects have an internal look-alike property called self-similarity. For instance, if we could look at the vessels of the heart with the naked eye and then through a microscope, we could not tell the difference. The large vessels branch into small vessels, which branch into smaller ones. At every magnification, in ever finer detail, the structures repeat themselves exactly. This is part of the hidden architecture of nature.

Fractal geometry has revealed what has always been there, beneath the surface of appearances, awaiting our discovery.

Stephane Mallarme wrote of life's "mysterious armature." Were we endowed with fiber optic vision, we might be able to detect the hidden frame. But we are marooned halfway between an atom and the sun, oblivious to the architectures at either end of the scale. As the rabbis found in the book of Numbers, so science has found in the realm of nature: what seems to be random may well be intended; what seems chaotic may well be designed; what seems to be aimless may well have a purpose beyond what we can discern. Whether from the Torah or from life itself, we are still learning the ultimate order of things, still discovering a precision and beauty we never invented and never imagined. Perhaps it is enough, as Anthony Hecht has written,

> to notice merely what is there...
> Some shadowless, unfocused light
> In which all things come into their own right...
> To be here now, and manifest
> The deep, unvexed composure of the blessed.

Camera obscura

Harry Golden, the late Jewish humorist, once related an insight that came to him while dining out. At the next table, he overheard a man giving the waitress a hard time because she mixed up his order. Golden pondered the lasting significance of the issue at hand. "When you think," he writes, "that there are at least four billion suns in the Milky Way, which is just one of billions of galaxies spaced about one million light years apart; and that the further you go into space, the thicker the galaxies become.... When you think of all this, isn't it kind of silly to worry whether the waitress brought you string beans instead of limas?"

But we do worry. Such concerns occupy, and sometimes even dictate, our lives. Unlike the philosopher Spinoza, we are not accustomed to see things *sub specie aeternitatis*, from the aspect of eternity. We are not philosophers with the leisure to reflect. We are too busy with the rush and crush of the everyday, the evanescent, the fleeting moments that somehow accumulate into lifetimes. To keep one's eye on eternity is not an easy task. Yet, as Joshua Loth Liebman observed, things which seem foolish in the light of eternity are probably foolish in themselves. To pass each day occupied only with the niggling details of life, ignoring its ultimate purpose, seems a little like chasing shadows with our backs to the light.

According to the Torah, the prophet Moses longed to see this light, to look upon the face of eternity. Having served God so faithfully for so long, he asks for this reward: "If I have found favor in Thy sight, show me now Thy Ways, that I may know Thee." God replies: "Thou canst not see My face, for man shall not see Me and live. But behold: there is a place next to Me; station thyself upon the rock."

What happened next is a subject of dispute among the commentators. Just what did Moses see? A nineteenth-century German rabbi, Samson Raphael Hirsch, explains it this way: Moses did not actually see God; rather he was permitted to see as God sees. It is the difference between looking into God's eyes, so to speak, and looking out of them. Moses was empowered, for a celestial moment, to see from a divine elevation, *sub specie aeternitatis*. As a reward for his loyal service to God, he was granted the rare vision of what truly matters, and what, like the difference between string beans and limas, doesn't.

There are moments when we too are granted such a vision, if from a lesser altitude. It may happen at those watershed moments in a lifetime: a wedding, when two lives are hallowed in joy; the birth of a child, when the promise of life seems infinite; or in the house of mourning, when the sorrow of bereavement may also confer the blessing of perspective. Yet it is not only at these milestones that we may glimpse eternity. Such moments of vision can come to us at the most prosaic times.

Years ago I was playing with my children in their bedroom. One of my daughters was sitting next to me on the floor with a book called *The Red Balloon*. As I played with the other children, I heard her talking happily about this balloon and the little boy who lost it and went everywhere looking for it. I thought she was doing what she had always done from her earliest years: making up her own story suggested by the pictures. Then I glanced at the book and the words on the page. It took several moments for it to dawn on me that she wasn't making up the words this time; she was *reading* them, reading a mile a minute. I was astonished: when did she learn to read? When did this miracle happen? At that moment, it was as though a veil had been lifted. I saw that my daughter was growing up before my oblivious eyes. I saw the impress of time upon her and felt its hand upon me. For that instant I saw from the higher elevation, like the rock where Moses stood.

It happens to all of us. One day you gaze at your son and realize that, while you were not looking, he has grown taller than you are. Or you see your daughter in her first prom dress and suddenly realize that, while you were not looking, she has blossomed into a woman. What we call time, Abraham Heschel once said, is merely eternity in disguise.

But we get only glimpses of it. The limits of our vision may be compared to a *camera obscura,* a tented chamber for viewing images. One steps inside and sets a piece of paper at a certain angle to an aperture. The view framed by the lens is reflected on the paper, and one can then trace the outline. But the sketch is three times removed from the subject: it is an outline of an image that is itself a mere reflection. If Moses glimpsed eternity, it may well have been as through a *camera obscura;* as if, in Bialik's phrase, one kissed a bride through a veil.

Yet as Moses learned, that is enough. To behold even a glimpse of light is to know that there is a light. And to see a deep impression on the anvil is to know that a mighty hand tends the forge.

the ear so magnified

SILVER TRUMPETS

WHILE WE MODERNS tend to confine God to the realm of theory, our ancestors did not. To them God was no mere concept but a source of irresistible power whose force they beheld all around and felt deep within. Unlike those of us today who cannot seem to find God anywhere, they knew exactly where He was. The Torah is remarkably specific about this. It describes God's presence as a cloud hovering over the Israelites. "On the day that the tabernacle was set up, the cloud covered the tent of the testimony, and in the evening it rested over the tabernacle in the likeness of fire until morning. It was always so: the cloud covered it, appearing as fire by night. Whenever the cloud would lift from the tent, the Israelites would set forward."

Seeing the cloud, of course, is not to be confused with seeing God, who has no form or image. A careful reading of the Torah account reveals that hearing is the critical faculty for perceiving God. The revelation at Sinai is auditory. When Moses invokes the divine name, he asks the people not to see but to "*Hear,* O Israel, the Lord is our God, the Lord is one."

The evidence of our eyes is not enough. This may explain why, as the Torah reports, God is not content to furnish the visual sign of the cloud. He also commands Moses to fashion two silver trumpets for the priests to sound in the hearing of all Israel. Whenever the cloud lifted, the trumpets were sounded. In this way the people would see and hear that God had summoned them forward.

Jewish tradition considers it a great honor to sound the ram's horn before the congregation at the New Year. Yet it is curious how the rabbis describe the obligation. "It is a positive act incumbent upon every Jew on this day," writes Maimonides, "to hear the blast of the ram's horn." The commandment is not to make the sound but to hear it. The Talmud emphasizes this distinction with the following hypothetical case. Imagine that the ram's horn was sounded over a deep cavity in the earth, so that both a blast and an echo were heard. In such an event, the rabbis decide, those standing down in the pit have fulfilled the commandment, for although they never saw the ram's horn, they heard its real sound. But those up above have not fulfilled their duty, for even though they actually saw the horn sounded, they heard only its echo. The obligation is to hear and to hear truly. It does not matter to the rabbis if the sound is pleasing to the ear. All sounds emitted by the ram's horn are valid, as long as the real sound is heard. The most important ritual commandment to be performed at the New Year is accomplished not by praying but by listening.

Perhaps the ability to hear—the true sound, not merely the echo—is considered so important just because it is so rare. According to a famous rabbinic midrash, when God decided to give the Torah, He went around to all the peoples of the earth, begging them to take it. But the nations did not hear, or could not, or would not, even when God Himself was speaking. None of them accepted the Torah. At last it was given to Israel. By this interpretation, the miracle was not that God called to Moses from the burning bush. The miracle was that Moses heard Him.

I still recall a telephone call I received years ago. The caller did not ask for anyone in particular. "Can I help you?" I said in that neutral tone that suggests the offer is less than heartfelt. The voice on the other end was a woman's. She began to talk about her son. Apparently he had left home as a teenager. She had not seen him in eleven years. She began to talk about his prayer shawl that she still kept for him. Then she described the prayer shawl worn by her father, who had died. Her father used to take her for walks when she was a little girl. He used to buy her caramels. Every time she tastes a caramel she remembers her father.

Ten minutes passed this way. (I know because I was looking at my watch.) At first I thought that she might be leading up to the reason for her call, but she never seemed to get there. Finally I decided that the conversation had gone on long enough. I interrupted her with my most imperious, "How can I be of help to you?" There was a pause at her end of the line. I thought: now I've hurt her feelings. I was sorry. But it was too late.

"Forgive me," she said. "You've been very kind. Thank you, thank you for listening to me." And she hung up. I couldn't call her back. I never asked for her number. I didn't even know her name.

Here was someone wanting merely for someone else to hear, someone to listen, even a disembodied stranger. And I heard her voice, but that was all. So concerned was I with the question I was waiting for that I missed the one she was asking: Will anyone listen to me?

There are other more casual, routine ways that we abuse our capacity to hear. In a culture that worships convenience and expediency, time is often too precious for the tedious task of listening. At the Beverly Hills Pharmacy, for instance, newspapers report that you can buy a bilingual note pad called "Tell-a-Maid." The notes consist of preprinted orders to Spanish-speaking domestic workers: *Lave el lavabo,* clean the sink. *Cambie la ropa,* change the sheets. *Limpie esto,* clean this. *Esto no lo toque,* don't touch that. The author of this innovation claims that she is doing a good deed. "It simplifies communication," she says, "so that you don't have to verbalize. It's mostly for people who aren't home when their help comes or don't have time to explain what they want."

Notice the author's choice of words: "people" are those who leave the notes, "help" are those who get them. Tell-a-Maid is designed to eliminate the necessity of contact between the two. If you leave these notes, you need never talk to the maid, let alone listen to her. The avowed purpose of Tell-a-Maid is not to teach Spanish but to avoid learning it. The goal is not to encourage conversation but to do away with it entirely. The last thing Tell-a-Maid asks you to do is to hear this person, to listen. It gives orders; it accepts no replies. Tell-a-Maid never asks, "How is your family?" or "Don't you feel well?" because it doesn't want to know. Apparently, neither do the "people" who leave the notes for the "help." Tell-a-Maid has proven so popular that a sequel has appeared: Tell-a-Gardener.

Even when we try to hear, even when we think we are listening to someone else, we are often listening only to ourselves. Our children can testify to this. How often they could rightfully complain, as one teenager is said to have complained to his school counselor: "You know what I am? I'm a comma. When I talk to my dad, he listens for a minute, then he starts talking. When I try to talk, he interrupts me. Well... not always. But even when he doesn't interrupt, he doesn't hear me either. As soon as I'm finished, he starts in right where he left off. He makes me a comma. It's as if I didn't say anything."

Stephen Vincent Benet once said that life is not lost by dying; it is lost hour by hour, minute by minute (and comma by comma), in all the thousand uncaring ways. What could be more obvious than the human need to be heard? What could be more essential to human dignity than the right to be acknowledged? Yet each of us, at one time or another, has felt like a comma. Each of us has felt the sting of indifference to what we say or what we feel, even as our own heedlessness has stung others. Nothing would seem more automatic than letting our ears do what they are meant to do. But this kind of hearing is not automatic. It requires more of the heart than of the eardrums.

The Russian writer Chekhov tells a story of a cab driver and his old horse. They are parked on the street on a cold winter night. The driver has yet to have one fare. Both he and his horse, covered by drifting snow, appear almost like ghosts. Finally a man hails the cab driver and shouts his destination. After they have been traveling for a while, the driver turns to his passenger and says, "Did you know, sir, my son died this week."

"Oh?" the passenger replies. "What did he die of?"

The driver begins to tell him, but the passenger is cold and in a hurry. "Listen," the passenger says, "can you hurry up a bit?"

Later on the driver picks up another fare, three young men. After waiting for a break in their conversation, he says to them, "My son ... died this week."

"Yes, we must all die," says one of the young men, resenting the intrusion. And the passengers return to their conversation.

The cab arrives at its destination, the passengers depart, and the cab driver is alone once more. It is late at night. No one else is about. He decides to return his horse to the stable for the night. Inside he sits in a warm corner and begins to talk with another driver.

"Listen, friend," he says, "you know, my son is dead.... Did you hear? This week, in the hospital.... It's a long story." But no sooner does he begin to tell it than he sees that the other driver is asleep.

Finally he walks over to where his horse is standing in its stall. The cab driver says, "You know, old horse, my son died this week." And he pours out his heart ... to the horse.

It is a sad story. Like many sad stories, there is too much

truth in it. Too often, no one hears the call of the lonely soul. No one hears the sound of the breaking heart.

Our biblical ancestors were blessed. God was real to them and near to them. They heard the silver trumpets. They heard when God was calling them. But they were listening.

It hurts

ONE SATURDAY AFTERNOON I was called to the county hospital. There was a patient there who they thought was Jewish, although there was no family to confirm it. The patient was dying. He was barely conscious. On my way to the hospital I steeled myself for the ordeal to come. I rehearsed the prayers to recite. I did not know this man. I never would.

I found him in the ward reserved for the indigent. The groaning and whimpering of the patients was a chorus of agony, what one might dream of hearing in the corridors of hell. I walked up to the patient. His eyes were open but showed no sign of recognition. I asked him if he had any family. No reply. I touched his hand. No response. I fumbled for a word of comfort. I recited the confession for the dying. He did not seem to hear me.

That's it, I said to myself. I've done my duty. I turned to leave when I heard him say something. He said it again, but I couldn't make it out. I had to put my ear right next to his mouth. What he was saying was: "It hurts."

These two words haunt me still. Whether or not they were spoken to me, they pierced me to the heart. It hurts to die all by yourself in a squalid bed. It hurts when no one is close enough to hear you. It hurts when there is no one who cares enough to feel your pain.

Rebbe Moshe Leib of Sassov said that he learned the meaning of love from a conversation he overheard between two old men.

"Tell me, my friend," said the first. "Do you love me?"

"Of course I love you," replied the second.

"Then tell me what hurts me," said the first.

"But how should I know what hurts you?" replied the second.

The first old man looked at his friend. "How can you say you love me," he demanded, "when you don't know what hurts me?"

Dorothea Soelle, the German theologian, has described our culture's compulsion to avoid this knowledge. She points out that in certain respects it is easy. The privation that is the daily lot of millions is no longer felt by most of us. The world we know is sealed airtight against hunger and cold. Starving children appear only on television, and only for a moment. We do not hear them cry out to us. We do not hear them say, "It hurts." As long as suffering is sufficiently remote, it is conveniently forgotten.

But this kind of indifference exacts a price. Apathy, as Soelle notes, is a Greek word that literally means "unable to feel." It means that one does not want to be touched, involved, drawn in. This is how struggling marriages are smoothly terminated, how the ties that bind generations are quickly dissolved, how the sick are removed from the house and the dead from the mind. This is how the curve of our life flattens out, until even joy does not elate us, even love does not move us. Ours becomes a world without seasons where, in the words of Kahlil Gibran, we laugh, but not all of our laughter, and weep, but not all of our tears. Only then, having so carefully steered clear of all pain, do we find that we have steered clear of life itself.

Given the comforts most of us enjoy and the interests we defend, it is easy enough to turn a deaf ear to the pain of others—not that such deafness is intended. Like novocaine, we numb our compassion, nerve by nerve, until at last we put our souls to sleep. But it is then, when we are most oblivious to pain, that we become most capable of inflicting it.

The Yiddish writer Isaac Loeb Peretz relates the tale of a wagon driver and his horse. The two were always at odds. The horse would say: "First feed me the oats, and then I will pull the wagon." The driver would answer: "First pull the wagon, and then I will feed you the oats." The driver was the one with the whip, and he would use it until the horse gave in. Finally the horse dropped dead.

Now the driver was forced to pull the wagon by himself. This was work for a horse, not a man. It took more strength than the driver had, and soon he too collapsed and died.

When the driver arrived before the Heavenly Court, he was informed that the horse had filed a complaint against him. He was summoned to appear for a *din Torah,* a hearing before the Throne of Judgment.

The horse testified: "He beat me unmercifully! He thrashed the life out of me with his whip!"

The driver retorted: "He's just a horse, and not much of a horse at that. Why, I saved his hide from the skinner! I only used the whip because he wouldn't move!"

"But I hadn't the strength!" cried the horse.

"Did I have the strength!" shouted the driver. "I had to pull the wagon myself. Is a horse not stronger than a man?"

The Heavenly Court was in a quandary. It deliberated quite a while before rendering its verdict: "The horse will not listen to the driver, and the driver will not listen to the horse. Therefore our sentence is: both of them will return to earth. The horse will become a driver, and the driver will become a horse. The Heavenly Court will wait until they learn to hear each other's voice and learn to feel each other's pain."

And the Heavenly Court is still waiting.

NINE WORDS

LEXICOGRAPHERS ESTIMATE that there are one million words in the English language, half of them in various stages of oblivion. Each person's vocabulary, of course, is only a fraction of that. The average recognition vocabulary (words understood when listening or reading) is thirty thousand words, the average use vocabulary (words used in speaking or writing) ten thousand words. But here is the surprising statistic: one-fourth of all spoken and written English requires only nine words. Nine words!

This claim seems preposterous on the face of it, but it has been corroborated many times. Recently I read a magazine article in which the writer proved it to himself. At random he selected an assortment of texts from around his house: everything from *Alice in Wonderland* to an automobile warranty, from a cookbook to the Boy Scout oath. He subjected these to a methodical and somewhat skeptical investigation, only to find that even this random sample showed the numbers to be astonishingly accurate: one-fourth of all the texts consisted of nine little words.

Without prolonging the suspense, here they are, in alphabetical order: and, be, have, it, of, the, to, will, you. That's it. Nothing earth-shattering here; but a few observations come to mind. Notice that "please" and "thank you" are missing, which may not be surprising; but notice also that the pronoun "I" is missing, which is surprising indeed. When you think about it, the nine words do manage to accomplish a great deal. The borders of human experience are virtually encompassed: existence (be), objects (it), others (you), past (have), and future (will). It is remarkable how much of reality can be compressed within such small margins.

But what I find most impressive is just how unimpressive the words are, how small. When we listen to others speaking, these are the last words we hear. When we read them on the page, they are the last ones we notice. When we say them aloud, we never pause to think about them. We think instead of the important words, the big ones, the powerful nouns. But none of these words is a noun. In fact, each is powerless by itself. Each of the nine words needs other words to communicate. Each is a helper, a connector. Without these little words you can bring up a subject, but you cannot pursue it. You can start a conversation, but you cannot finish it. More spectacular words may clamor for attention, but these, the least imposing, least obvious, least audible—these are the bedrock of our language. These bind thought to thought. These make speech possible.

What is true of our language is true of our lives. As much as we might think of ourselves as the powerful nouns, the subject of the sentence and the title of the story, we never stand in splendid isolation. The Torah, too, seems to know this. There we find the song of hope uttered by Moses before his death. Scholars have noticed that the poem has a triangular construction: the three vectors of God, Israel, and the world as a whole. Each depends on the actions of the others. The omnipotent God who says, "I deal death and give life; none can deliver from My hand," is the same God who is also described as an eagle bearing His nestlings aloft on His wings. When they stray from Him, He is aggrieved; when they desert Him, He is bereft. There can be no noun more powerful than God, yet not even God can stand alone.

Without the ties that bind us to each other, we too are as bereft as a lonely God and as helpless as human speech. The nine little words remind us of what our hearts already know: that we need each other; that our lives, like our words, thrive on connection; and that, sometimes, what is least apparent is also what is most important.

INFRASOUND

THROUGHOUT THE TORAH are found the familiar words, "And God spoke to Moses saying...." The formula is so commonplace that one tends to overlook it. What does it mean? Did God actually speak to Moses with a voice? If so, did He sound like a human being? If so, how did Moses know it was God? And if there was no voice—if Moses merely understood God's word by some telepathic process—then why does the text always say, "And God *spoke*"?

The Jewish sages posed these questions long ago. Their attention was drawn in particular to a verse from the book of Exodus. Describing the construction of the ark of the covenant, the God of Israel specifies exactly where His voice will be heard: "... from above the cover on top of the ark between the two cherubim; there will I meet with you, and there will I speak to you." The cherubim, as the Torah explains elsewhere, were a pair of winged figures of gold designed to shield the ark. It was precisely from between the cherubim, above the ark, that Moses heard God's voice.

But how could it be, asked the sages, that this divine voice—the voice that, in the words of the Psalmist, shatters the cedars of Lebanon, makes the mountains leap and the deserts tremble—how could such a voice be inaudible to those outside the tent of the tabernacle? We might think that God was merely whispering, but the sages point out that the text uses the same expression in this passage that is used to describe the thunderous voice at Sinai. One rabbinic midrash suggests that the voice was the same as always, but when it reached the entrance of the tent it miraculously ceased. Another version has it that the voice came to Moses from heaven through a tube of fire so that it was audible only to him.

It is true that the mechanics of revelation were of more interest to the sages than they are to us. They believed with utter certitude that God spoke to Israel. We moderns, on the other hand, live in an age suspicious, if not contemptuous, of such things. God does not seem to speak to us anymore. Since the destruction of the ancient Temple, says the Talmud, only children and madmen converse with God. The rest of us, it would seem, are destined never to hear the divine voice, whether a roar or a whisper.

Still, there is reason to wonder: could it be that God is still speaking to us, that He has been speaking to us all along, only from a place outside the tent, in a language we do not expect, a language too various, too wonderful to understand?

This thought occurred to me when learning about the phenomenon of infrasound. Scientific research confirms that the universe is filled with sounds we do not hear. The human capacity to perceive sound is limited to the equivalent of nine octaves, a considerable but by no means comprehensive range. Beyond those nine octaves is a subsonic frequency that instruments can detect, even if our ears cannot. Massive movements of earth, air, fire, and water are not silent. What we hear of an earthquake, or of thunder, or of a volcano, is only a sliver of the total sound. Likewise we hear the impact of an ocean wave, but not the wave itself. We hear raindrops when they collide with the roof, but not when they fall through the air. The range of human hearing comprehends birds and frogs, but not porpoises and bats. A bat's echolocation, for instance, is sensitive enough to register a beetle walking on sand or a moth flexing its wings. If the natural world can be compared to a grand symphony, we are hearing only traces of the music.

Could it be much the same with the language of God? Perhaps we are simply not aware of, or alive to, all of the divine lexicon, all of its forms and expressions. Perhaps nature has its own liturgy, a divine language in the light of dawn, in the stars and ocean tides, in the outburst of spring and the laughter of children. Are not all of these words of God, written on the parchment of our days? Walt Whitman wrote:

> I find letters from God dropt in the street, and everyone
>   is sign'd by God's name,
> And I leave them where they are, for I know that
>   wheresoe'er I go,
> Others will punctually come for ever and ever.

Another writer, Frederick Buechner, calls it the alphabet of grace, the sounds that are not shouted but whispered: the hum of bees and the rush of the wind, words of love in the dark, the hiss of whitecaps over glittering sand, even the sound of our own breath. It is the sound, he says, of our lives trying to tell us something, of a whole world crying out in tongues.

Are we listening?

ME, MYSELF, AND I

WHILE THE TORAH is not often compared to music, it carries a phrase that is a kind of refrain. This phrase recurs after divine injunctions. For example: "The priests shall not profane the sanctuary; I am the Lord. They shall not profane My holy name; I am the Lord. They shall keep My charge; I am the Lord. I will be hallowed among the Israelites; I am the Lord. You shall not neglect the poor; I am the Lord. You shall treat the stranger with justice; I am the Lord."

So goes the refrain: *I am the Lord.* But why the constant repetition? After all, each paragraph of the Law already begins with the words, "And the Lord spoke to Moses...." We know who is speaking. There can be no mistaking the voice of God. Nor could the rabbis believe that divine speech was ever redundant. Every word of the Torah is necessary. How, then, to explain the refrain of "I am the Lord," repeated and repeated even though we have already heard it?

Because we haven't heard it. Because we live our lives as if it were not so. Because we refuse to acknowledge God, to hear Him or to heed Him. Because, as Maimonides wrote some eight hundred years ago, "The intent of the entire Torah is to put an end to idolatry," yet we persist in the idolatry of our own age, the idolatry of self. God must say to us, again and again, "I am the Lord," because we act as if *we* are. We are incapable of hearing His voice because we are too enamored of ours. We are like the little child on the telephone, dialing the only number she knows and getting a busy signal. Again and again God says, "I am the Lord," but we can't hear Him. Our line is always busy, declaring ourselves.

If the word "self" were a stone and our sentences were pathways, we could barely walk without stumbling. The pages of popular books, magazines, and television shows are littered with self: express yourself, fulfill yourself, actualize yourself, feel good about yourself. The self-improvement industry, like McDonald's, has developed franchises, hamburger stands of the soul. I have heard this trend described by a popular comedian. Once, he says, we subscribed to *Life* magazine, but that was too broad a subject. So we narrowed it down to *People,* but who cares about all of them? So we shrunk it down still further to *Us,* getting closer to our true desire; and then the final, inevitable step: *Self* magazine, the perfect title for our times, the open homage to our rock and our redeemer. One of the most popular songs of recent years has this refrain: "Learning to love yourself is the greatest love of all." Do we not believe it? Is this not become our religion?

Even in the rarefied heights of higher learning, the new faith prevails. Consider, as an example, recent research of the Renaissance period. William Shakespeare and Leonardo da Vinci were perhaps its two greatest figures. Each left a lasting mark on the course of Western civilization. Each of their works is still studied with minute attention by those seeking to unlock the mysteries of genius. Just recently, scholars have claimed two dramatic breakthroughs, one concerning the sonnets of Shakespeare and the other Leonardo's most famous portrait.

First, a methodological note. In recent years it has been recognized that no critic of the past can be wholly objective in the present. That is, no one assessing the prejudices of another day is entirely free of his or her own. The Hebrew Bible is a case in point. We moderns know it as a book among others. For the ancients, however, it was a communication from God which they regarded with awe. Readers of today can rarely read the Bible in the same way. Our reaction is inevitably conditioned by the attitudes of our own time. So also with Shakespeare or Leonardo: their works arose in a vastly different era, and what we see in them has as much to do with our lives as with theirs.

This may explain what the scholars found. First, concerning Shakespeare: one of the longest-lived debates in literary history involves the identity of a mysterious Mr. W. H. to whom Shakespeare's sonnets were dedicated in 1609. Over the years, hundreds of books and articles have speculated whether W. H. was a publisher, a friend, a lover, etc. Researchers were never able to agree, but now a young American professor has announced that he has solved the mystery: W. H., he claims, is merely a misprint. It should have been W. S.—Shakespeare really dedicated his sonnets to . . . himself!

Scholars have also wondered, for centuries now, who the woman was who posed for Leonardo's Mona Lisa. Was it a patron or a peasant, a daughter, a relative, a friend, a lover? Now it is claimed that this mystery, too, has at last been solved. An enterprising researcher compared a portrait of the artist with the portrait of Mona Lisa, measuring the sizes of the eyes, nose, mouth, and forehead of the two figures and the distances between them. Here is his verdict: the Mona Lisa is none other than the artist in disguise. Leonardo's most famous painting is a furtive picture of . . . himself!

Of course, neither of these two theories has yet been proven to anyone's satisfaction, and the two debates are probably not over. What interests me is not whether the theories are correct but what they have in common. Has anyone, let alone the greatest writer of his time, ever dedicated his poems to himself? Was Leonardo secretly so preoccupied with his own face? Yet if it is true that theories about the past are really descriptions of the present, we see what the present is all about: the self, or as we used to say as children, "Me, myself and I." *We* are the Lord, not God.

But that refrain is not found in the Torah, where learning

to love yourself is *not* the greatest love of all. It is the commandment of our own age. The Torah's message has to do with a still greater love, the one we give with all our hearts, with all our souls and all our might; the one turned outward, not inward; the love of God, not of ourselves.

In the Torah, when Moses sings, these are the words: "The Lord is my strength and song, and He is become my salvation."

Not now

O NE OF MY FAVORITE HAUNTS is the children's corner of a local bookstore. For readers of any age, there is no end of pleasure to be found there and no want of wisdom. Among my favorites is a book called *Not Now, Bernard* by David McKee. Here is the story it tells (regrettably, without the pictures).

Bernard's father was hammering a nail.

"Hello, Dad," said Bernard.

"Not now, Bernard," said his father.

Bernard's mother was fixing dinner.

"Hello, Mom," said Bernard.

"Not now, Bernard," said his mother.

"There's a monster in the garden, and it's going to eat me," said Bernard.

"Not now, Bernard," said his mother.

Bernard went into the garden. There was a monster, and the monster ate Bernard up. Then the monster went into the house.

Bernard's mother was cleaning the kitchen. The monster sneaked up behind her and roared. But she did not turn around. "Not now, Bernard," she said.

Bernard's father was reading the newspaper. The monster roared at him too, but he did not look up. "Not now, Bernard," he said.

Bernard's mother put his dinner in front of the television. After a while she called out from the next room, "Time for bed." The monster went upstairs and got into Bernard's bed. In a few minutes Bernard's mother walked by the room, reached in to turn off the light, and closed the door.

"But I'm a monster!" cried the monster.

And through the door the monster heard her say: "Not now, Bernard."

The moral of the story, while unstated, is hardly uncertain. How many times, in the midst of some urgent task, have we been interrupted by the insistent tug of a child's hand— "Mommy come look, Daddy come see!"—only to respond with a weary, "Not now, Bernard." As if there will always be another time, a better time. How often have we failed to hear the voices of those closest to us and most precious to us?

In the Torah, if not in our lives, God announces His revelations. Paragraph after paragraph begins with, "The Lord spoke to Moses...." Sometimes it is as though God is waking Moses up: "Moses, Moses!" Why, ask the rabbis, does God say the name twice? Would not once have been enough? Moses was not hard of hearing. Perhaps it is because the message is especially urgent. Or perhaps it is because even those with the most acute hearing are not always listening. Even Moses was not always paying attention. To attune one's perception to the score of revelation, in all its surpassing glory, is a gift even prophets may lack.

Years ago I lived in an apartment with walls like paper. My neighbors always had their television on late into the night, and I could hear every word. There was no use complaining; the problem was with the walls, not the television. At first the noise prevented sleep. But after a few nights it merely delayed it; within a week or two, I barely even noticed the sound. It had become a kind of white noise, like the traffic in the street or the hum of the refrigerator. One doesn't hear those sounds until they cease. And sure enough, that is what happened: the neighbors moved out. All of the sudden it was too quiet to sleep. I yearned for the sound of their television. Realizing that I had come to hear it without noticing it, I wondered: To what else have I become deaf? What else was I taking for granted?

This brings me back to "Not now, Bernard," to all the ways we ignore the sound of God calling to us. When a moment is given to notice, or to share, and we say, "Not now," we depreciate what little time we have. We reduce today to a rehearsal for tomorrow. While we were waiting anxiously for the sound of the doorbell, announcing the expected guest, he was already in the house. He stayed for a while, and then he left, and we never even knew he was there.

The Sadagora rebbe and one of his students were waiting for a train. Said the rebbe: "There is divine wisdom in everything, not only in what God created in the beginning, but in what we invent today. Everything has something to teach us about the ways of God."

The student was dubious. "So what can we learn from a telegraph?" he asked.

"From the telegraph we learn that every word is counted and charged."

"And the telephone?"

"That what we say here is heard there."

So immersed in their discussion were the rebbe and the student that they did not hear the conductor calling the passengers. Finally they noticed that the train was leaving. They ran for the last car but just missed it. After they caught their breath, the student ruefully asked the rebbe: "And what can we learn from the train?"

"From the train," replied the rebbe, "we learn that because of one second, one can miss everything."

All too often, one does. "Not now, Bernard," we say. But the sages, in four of their most famous words, ask: "If not now, when?"

THE SILENT LETTER

IN THE SOUTHERN PART of the Sinai peninsula is a mountain which the Bedouin call Gebel Musa, the mountain of Moses. Although modern scholarship considers it doubtful that this mountain is the Horeb mentioned in the Torah, nonetheless it is revered as the traditional site.

It is hard to imagine a more remote place than Gebel Musa. Equidistant from the Gulf of Elat and the Gulf of Suez, it is one of the most forbidding landscapes on earth. On my visit there years ago, there were no roads. The only modern transport available was a military truck with seats bolted to the flatbed. The driver maneuvered the truck down the desert *wadis*. Occasionally we had to get out and push a wheel over a rock or through a sand drift. There was no life that we could see, not even a footprint. It could have been the moon.

Finally we reached Gebel Musa. At the foot of the mountain is a monastery called Santa Katerina, where pilgrims may stay over. Exhausted from our journey and the brutal sun, we trooped into an enclosed courtyard. There we were informed that a number of monks made their permanent homes in the monastery. As their guests, we were requested to respect the rules of their various religious orders. Quiet would be particularly appreciated, since the monks were unaccustomed to the clamor of conversation.

There in that terrible wilderness, standing in the crushing desert heat, my respect for monastic renunciation knew no bounds. But I remember thinking: is it not enough that these men spend their lives here, utterly cut off from the world? Must they also be cut off from us? Must they also renounce the warmth of the spoken word, the embrace of the human voice?

The ascetic or monastic impulse is not unknown to Judaism. Two thousand years ago, a group of Jews settled in a remote place called Qumran, on the shores of the Dead Sea. There they lived in celibacy and seclusion, believing that the world was about to end and awaiting the messiah. We know that this group existed only because their library of scrolls somehow survived. But their preference for isolation, to our knowledge, did not include silence. In Jewish tradition, speech is essential to the order of being. Creation began with words: God spoke, and it was. The first divine encounters were auditions, not visions. What Elijah heard was "a still, small voice." The Qumran community lived in solitude but not in silence, for the source of their faith was the spoken word.

Where human beings are absent, it is different. Above the earth's atmosphere, the heavens are silent. No sound is heard in the vacuum of space. Planets spin, meteors flame, stars explode: we hear nothing. Yet for all its mystery, the miracle of creation is not this primeval silence but the voice that breaks it, that reaches to us across the void. Silence is awe, but speech is holy. In the synagogue, even silent devotions are repeated aloud, as if God Himself prefers speech to silence.

If the Sinai monks would have spoken to us, they might have told us what silence can teach. Lying on a cot that night in the monastery, it was as if I heard, for the first time, the recesses of the night: the fastness of stone, the soughing of wind, the far sweep of the desert sand. Silence magnifies the audible. It summons us to wakefulness. It instructs us in the art of hearing beyond the commotion of mortal tongues. The book of Leviticus begins with the verse, "The Lord called to Moses." In Hebrew, the first word is *vayyiqra*, a form of the verb "to call." Curiously, in Torah scrolls the final letter of this word, *alef*, is always written in a smaller hand, as if it were almost forgotten. Indeed, it is easy to forget the *alef*: it is a silent letter, having no sound except that of the closest vowel. Yet were it not for the *alef*, the meaning of the word *vayyiqra* would be lost, and the Lord could no longer call to Moses, or to us. The difference between hearing God and not hearing Him is an inaudible letter. Even silence can speak.

Yet the asceticism of the monastery is not the Jewish path to God. Such detachment leads too far away from the shared tasks of living. There is a story from the Hasidic tradition about a zealous young student who wished to be ordained. He came before the rebbe seeking to demonstrate his piety. "I dress all in white," he said. "To mortify myself, I put nails in my shoes; I roll naked in the snow; I order the caretaker of the synagogue to lash me on my bare back; and I endure all this in silence." Just then, so the story goes, a white horse wandered past and began rolling around in the snow. "Look there," said the rebbe. "That creature is clad in white. It has nails in its shoes. It rolls around in the snow. It receives lashes on its bare back. It says nothing. But it is a horse."

In the Jewish religious tradition, as in others, there is a certain respect for the purifying power of self-denial, solitude, and silence. The privations of the desert can refine the spirit. But the desert is a station on the journey, not its destination. Among the ancient sages there was a tradition that when the messiah comes, he will dwell for a while in the desert outside Jerusalem. But God will not let him stay there. For God's concern is to be heard by the people, and the messiah is called to speak to them, and there are no people in the desert.

MISSING VOICES

A S A CHILD IN SCHOOL I was always happy to see sub-
stitute teachers, because they liked to pass the time by
showing films. If you knew how to thread the projector, they
might assign you to spend the whole day winding and rewind-
ing the reels. The films were wildly unpredictable. Most were
dreary fare (world geography, the life of Pasteur), though
some were exotic (ovoviparous reptiles, rare diseases) and a
few were even thrilling (human anatomy and reproduction).
But there was one film from my school days that I still recall
with piercing clarity.

It was a black and white newsreel from the "Third World,"
a place, I concluded, where no one would ever want to go. It
showed poverty in China, misery in India, famine in Africa.
It showed endless straggling columns of refugees, fleeing wars
or floods, staring uncomprehendingly into the camera. Their
faces, gaunt and haggard, were lined with pain. Sometimes
their lips were moving. But there was never any sound when
they spoke. The soundtrack did not record their voices. The
effect was eerie: whenever the newsreel focused on these
people, the film fell silent. It was as if they stood behind
glass, like specimens, like extraterrestrials. Whatever they
were saying, we couldn't hear it.

Yet if the Hebrew Scriptures have anything to teach us, it
is that God could hear it and hears it still. What the newsreel deleted, this God demands: the acknowledgment of our
common humanity; the divine dignity of each life; the right of

each voice to be heard. "And God heard their groaning, and God took notice of them." In the Scriptures, the soundtrack is not silent. Voices carry.

In an essay entitled "A Thousand Million Invisible Men," Shiva Naipaul has written of our illusion of the "Third World." He acknowledges that it is difficult to bridge the abyss between unimagined wealth and unimagined poverty, between those who eat three square meals every day and those who don't eat that many in a lifetime. But he argues that the term "Third World" is really a bloodless expedient that robs individuals and societies of their particularity, of their unique voice. We tend to think of the Third World as passive and silent, the skeletal receptacles of our largess. But Naipaul reminds us that each people, each person, is invested with unique and irreducible dignity. "People look alike," he remarks, "only when you can't be bothered to look at them closely." In truth, the Third World does not exist; it never did. Hundred of millions of people cannot be lumped into off-the-rack lots. The condition of three-quarters of humanity is more various, more complex, and more urgent than that. The Third World, Naipaul writes, is only a way of imposing anonymity, of making invisible, of reducing to silence.

Perhaps, in the ancient court of Pharaoh, this is what it was like. From the privileged distance of his throne and the luxuries of his palace, Pharaoh gazed upon his realm: his courtiers, his legions, his subjects; and at the furthest remove, if he bothered to look that far, he might even have glimpsed the Third World of his day, the nameless masses, the slow-moving files of refugees in stony landscapes. "And Pharaoh made their lives bitter with hard service, in mortar and in brick...and the children of Israel groaned by reason of their bondage, and they cried out." What did Pharaoh care? His was the power, the glory, the wealth, the comfort. Why should he notice them? Why should he care about them? Why should he hear their cries? Who would show him that each of that desolate multitude was a human being, a bearer of God's image, entitled by birth to a share of God's blessings?

We know who showed him. "And God heard their groaning… and God took notice of them." What Pharaoh would not hear, God would not silence. In every contest with the powerful, this God stands beside the powerless. If the Torah were a newsreel, Pharaoh would be the one aiming the camera. God would be the one staring into it, His face a sad reflection of our own.

*divine
things*

PERSPECTIVE

THIS IS THE STORY of my GTI. That is the model of the car I used to drive. It was a little black two-door sedan, like a hundred other subcompact cars on the road: a nondescript, generic hatchback, no chrome, no metallic paint, not the kind of car to attract attention. But my GTI attracted all kinds of attention. It was broken into, if memory serves, seven times.

There was a reason for this popularity. Unlike most cars, the GTI was not factory-equipped with a tape deck. That item was purchased from the dealer, and the dealer installed it. This meant that it was easy to install. It also meant that it was easy to remove. The thieves were not long in figuring this out. While they rip out the dashboard when necessary, they prefer ease and convenience like anyone else. That made the GTI a prime target.

The first time mine was robbed, the thief shattered the passenger window with what must have been a crowbar. I found a gum wrapper on the front seat: a relaxed thief. After that, in numbing succession, my GTI had its locks picked, its hood bent, and its door handles pried off. Once when I was out of town overnight, I left my GTI parked at the airport. By this time I had no tape deck. When I returned, I found the car held up by two jacks. The thieves, finding nothing to steal inside, had taken the wheels. The lug nuts were stacked very neatly on the roof of the car.

I tried to fight back. The first time, I even called the police.

But there seemed to be little they could do about this kind of crime. These days a car is either stolen, vandalized, or burglarized about as often as we breathe. One form of protection is a car alarm, but practiced thieves can disarm them in seconds. Another strategy is to get a removable tape deck. I tried this. The problem is that when the thieves see the empty slot in the dashboard, they break in anyway, because they figure the tape deck must be hidden under the seat or in the trunk. (I should know. That is where they found mine.) Some drivers have taken to putting signs in the car window: "No radio, no stereo." No luck. I read in the newspaper that one driver finally gave up and wrote: "Welcome."

On the urban frontier today, there seems to be no limit to what people will steal. In New York City, residents are chaining down their house plants. On the Upper East Side, landscapers are planting root balls under wire lattice and cabling six-foot trees to underground cinder blocks. On the Lower East Side, simple shrubs are guarded by barbed wire. Central Park's Conservatory Garden is now guarded by armed police.

It is disheartening. In the case of my GTI, I was angry and exasperated, particularly when I had to pay out the deductible to repair the damages. But in time, the succession of burglaries seemed almost inevitable, and I became inured, if not entirely resigned. After all, I told myself, this was a case of someone taking my property, not my life. A tape deck may be valuable, but it is not invaluable. How much anguish does the loss of this object deserve? How much exertion does its protection demand? How much time do we lavish upon the things we own, scheming how to acquire them, how to finance them, how to safeguard them? Our lives and our labors focus so fiercely upon our possessions that they become magnified in our sight. How many of us, when our property is stolen, feel as if we have been personally violated, as if our very selves have been robbed?

Yet in truth this is hardly the case. The thefts of my tape deck were impersonal affairs, having to do with the tape deck's value, not mine. It is important, it seems to me, to know the difference. It is important to keep our possessions in perspective. The Jewish sages have a saying: The more you own, the more you worry. Our possessions rarely warrant the anxiety we invest in them. They are, after all, only things. Unlike human relationships, they give nothing back. We can hold them in our hands, but they are cold to the touch.

Near the beginning of the book of Genesis is an account of how our ancient forebears built a tower that reached to the heavens. So displeased was God that He confused human language and dispersed the human race. The rabbis wondered: while the sins of Adam and Eve, or of Cain, or of the generation of the flood are clear enough, what was so terrible about the tower of Babel? Why did it provoke God's wrath?

In the rabbinic Midrash there is an explanation. It was not the tower itself that offended God, but the tower builders. The tower was made of bricks, and the builders were obsessed with them. In fact, a brick was more precious in their sight than a bricklayer. If he fell from the tower and met his death, they took little notice, because he was easy to replace. But if a brick fell from the tower, the builders wept, because it would take forever to carry up another one.

Does this not indeed merit God's indignation, to value bricks more than lives? And are we not, at times, like the ancient tower builders? Are we not also, too often, obsessed by bricks, by objects, by possessions? The TVs, CDs, VCRs, GTIs—this is the alphabet of the consumer culture. In our times, these things have assumed an almost spiritual value, as if they were a means of salvation. What is necessary is to accumulate more and more of them, and we have raised that necessity to a faith. A picture was once worth a thousand words; now it is worth a thousand dollars. Sometimes it seems like we are more concerned with the flow of cash than the flow of rivers. Sometimes it seems like we are more concerned with the flow of oil than the flow of blood.

The tendency to measure our happiness by our possessions has been confirmed by SRI International, a research firm that has devised a method of human classification called VALS, for "values and lifestyles." VALS categorizes human beings not by the qualities of their character but by the products in their refrigerator. You are what you buy. After evaluating our consumption habits and motivations, VALS can tell us whether we are survivors (one step removed from poverty); achievers (one block removed); emulators (achievers with little alligators on our shirts); or the ultimate accolade, satisfied selves. This is the ambition of the consumer culture: to equate what we have with what we are. Everywhere we are besieged by the same message: that the nature of life is to want things; the purpose of life is to buy things; the reward of life is to own things. Acquisition is justified as fulfillment, and greed as need. In the VALS universe, there is no difference between self-worth and net worth.

That is why the story of my GTI is not a tale of woe, but a lesson in perspective: not to grow too attached to the objects I own; to recognize that human attachments are the ones that deserve to be cherished.

I have always been struck by the familiar advertising slogan, "A diamond is forever." It may be true. A stone is more enduring than a person. The tower of Babel probably stood long after its builders had perished. Many of our own possessions are sure to outlast us. A diamond may be forever, but we are only for a little while. We spend so much of our time counting out coins. But in the end, it is our lives that have been spent.

HUMILITY

AMONG THE ANCIENT RABBIS, humility was considered to be a cardinal virtue. When describing the ideal attributes of the Jewish people, the Talmud elevates humility to the same stature as mercy and goodness. The sages believed that Israel was summoned by God precisely because it was the humblest of peoples in the humblest condition of servitude. They pointed out that even Almighty God chose to reveal Himself from the humblest of His creations, a lowly thornbush.

But humility does not come easily. The Scriptures repeatedly warn against the sin of "lifting our hearts above our brothers." The rabbis found it necessary to remind us, lest we become too haughty, that the worm preceded us in the order of creation. The Torah depicts the prophet Moses as the humblest, most modest man on the face of the earth, yet even he faltered at times. On one notable occasion, he actually denounces the Israelites and finds fault with God Himself: "Wherefore hast Thou dealt ill with Thy servant?" he demands. "Wherefore have I not found favor in Thy sight, that Thou layest the burden of all this people on me? Have I conceived them? Have I brought them forth? I am not able to bear all this people alone. And if Thou would deal thus with me, then kill me!"

If one reads this tirade sympathetically, one might conclude that Moses was simply venting his frustration with a refractory people. On the other hand, his outburst hardly becomes a man of humility. He acts as if the burden of leadership is his alone, as if he, and not God, is in charge. Was it Moses who inflicted the plagues upon Egypt? Was it Moses who freed the slaves? Was it Moses who divided the sea? All of this was the work of God. On what basis, then, does Moses complain that he is pulling the weight alone? He is merely the servant, not the master; the handwriting, not the hand. Yet he seems to confuse the two. Of course, he was not the first to do so, nor the last.

When it comes to vanity, not even Moses is beyond reprimand. A Hasidic teacher is reported to have said: "You may observe every commandment in the Torah; you may purify and perfect yourself by obeying every law; and yet, if at the last moment your perception is tainted by a single vain thought, you have ruined everything." This may be an exaggeration, but vanity is never far away, not even from the saints. The rabbis prized humility so highly precisely because it is found so rarely.

Lewis Lapham has described a recent phenomenon that shows how far we are estranged from the rabbinic preference for humility. He calls it "the magical property of celebrity." No longer is the craving for attention confined to entertainers. These days everyone wants to stand in front of the camera. Athletes show up on television, promoting whatever can be carried into a locker room. Businessmen star in their own commercials and commission their own biographies. Contemporary culture is entranced with notoriety, almost, as Lapham suggests, to the point of adoration. Actors pronounce ritual incantations over otherwise lifeless blue jeans, cameras, or cans of beer, thus making them fit for us to consume. Celebrities are the priesthood of the consumer religion.

One amusing example cited by Lapham bears repeating. It seems that on a New York City television station a few years ago, the weather reporter caught a cold. Apparently she was considered irreplaceable: the producers took their cameras to her bedside in Queens, from where she dutifully delivered the weather forecast, in between sniffles and sneezes. It was as if, without her, there could be no weather, that rain or snow would not exist unless she reported it. As Lapham writes, perhaps they believed it would rain for forty days and forty nights if their celebrity forecaster failed to make her evening invocation to the storm gods.

The same sort of thing happens during presidential elections or national crises. The news "anchors" stay in front of the camera hour after hour, as if nothing could happen without them there to authenticate it, as if the news were an aspect of their personality.

Or consider the way movies begin, with the list of credits. Here vanity is not a frailty but a law. The producer wants the "presentation credit." The idea is to have this placed above the "artwork title," while everyone else who worked on the picture falls below it. But there are problems when there is more than one producer. Whose name takes precedence? Everyone wants to be in the left-hand position, because they think their names will be read first. Producers bid on the right to appear in the left-hand position. "Special billing" goes to the lead actors, then shrinks a bit for the supporting cast, then shrinks again for the screenwriter, and again for the technicians. The exact size of the type is stipulated by contract to the millimeter. Major actors want their names to appear in type no smaller than the "follow title." At the very least, they insist upon the assurance that no other actor will get bigger type than theirs. When two major actors appear in the same movie, there can be major problems. Both are likely to want the favored left-hand position. A recently developed compromise awards one actor the left-hand position but places the name a notch lower than the right-hand name. But even this does not always work. In one case, neither actor would accept second billing, so their names were printed diagonally to form an X!

The movies, of course, are the last place to find humility.

Yet they are an index of our culture's values. The obsession with celebrity testifies to what can happen when all humility is lost. A sense of proportion departs with it. All that is left is a desperate scramble for a glory measured in millimeters.

Even Moses was not immune to the lure of celebrity. He too was seduced at times by his own importance. But the rabbis insist that it was his humility that recommended him. It was his readiness to revere, rather than his hunger to command, that qualified him to serve God. So the Talmud teaches: Whoever humbles himself, the Lord shall exalt; whoever exalts himself, the Lord shall humble.

A Torah scroll, in contrast to the movie credits, is written in a uniform hand. There are no capital letters. All the words are the same size. No name is written larger than any other: neither that of Moses, nor of God Himself.

Gratitude

THE DINER HAD JUST OPENED, and I was the only cus-
tomer. The proprietors, a Chinese couple who appeared
to be husband and wife, stood behind the counter. They
looked at me apprehensively. I ordered. The man said,
"Thank you." His wife was wiping my empty table, which
was already immaculate. They were trying so hard, and here
the place was empty. When the order arrived, I said, "Thank
you." *He* said, "Thank you." I hadn't even paid him yet. I
gave him a $10 bill. "Thank you," he said. He brought me
the change. "Thank you," he said. As I got up to leave, he
said, "Thank you." I said good-bye. He said, "Thank you."

I had gathered that "thank you" was the only thing this
man knew how to say in English. But then, that is quite a lot.
Maybe he didn't even know what these two words mean. But
then, maybe we don't either.

Abraham Joshua Heschel once said that humankind will
not perish for want of information but for want of appre-
ciation. Ours is not a grateful age. We who have more and
more complain louder and louder about less and less. Two out
of every three people on earth are chronically malnourished,
and we complain about the high cost of dining out. Twenty-
six nations have per capita incomes of less than $300 a year,
and we complain about our income tax. Thirty percent of the
children of these nations die before they are five years old,
and we complain because college tuition is too expensive. We
pass our days so preoccupied with ourselves that we fail to

see beyond ourselves. Our vision dims at the horizon of our own cares. We convert our desires into virtues until, having so often ruined joy with resentment, we wonder about the lack of tenderness in our own lives. The cold laws of convenience and material comfort make for a world of ice, where the soul can freeze to death.

A Hasidic tradition imagines visitors summoned by the king to a magnificent palace. The palace has many halls. In every one the visitors find a new treasure. At first they wonder how the treasures came to be there, but after a while they don't care; they are too busy filling their pockets. By the time they have finished, they no longer remember why they came to the palace in the first place. Meanwhile, at the end of the hallways, the king is still waiting for his visitors. He is still waiting for those of his subjects who think of him rather than of the treasure.

To say "thank you" is to think of the king and not merely of the treasure. What we have may be ours, but what we are is not ours. We did not create our own lives, nor did we earn them. They are ours only in trust, on loan, until the lender calls them in. Our sensation of self-sufficiency is an illusion. Every breath we take is borrowed. Every moment of love we know is but a fraction of a greater love, as surely as the stars we see are only a fraction of all the light there is.

The physician and writer Richard Selzer tells of a young woman who has just been wheeled out of surgery. Outside in the corridor, her husband is waiting. The surgeon walks over to them. "We removed the tumor," he says. "The surgery went well."

Something in the surgeon's eyes says that it did not go so well. "We had to sever a facial nerve to get at the growth. The nerve controls the muscles of the mouth."

There is a pause. Then the husband asks, "But otherwise she'll be okay?"

"Oh, yes," says the surgeon. "Other than that, she'll be perfectly fine."

The husband's eyes are alight with joy. "Thank God!" he cries. "I was afraid she.... Thank God!"

Later the nurses wheel her into her room. She is awake. Her husband gazes down at her. He sees that her mouth is twisted in a palsy. She asks him, "Will my mouth always be like this?"

He leans toward her and says very gently, "To remove the tumor in your cheek, they had to cut the nerve."

She nods and is silent. Tears well in her eyes.

But he smiles. "I like it," he says. Then, unmindful, he bends down to kiss her crooked mouth, and the physician who witnesses this can see how the young man twists his own lips to accommodate hers, to show her that their kiss still works.

Here is the power of gratitude: his for her life; hers for his love. To be grateful for both, to say "thank you" again and again, is a mighty thing, a divine thing. For only when we learn to feel gratitude for the gifts of life and love do we catch sight of their Giver.

Love

According to Rabbi Akiba, the greatest of all the ancient Jewish sages, the most important words that God ever uttered are these: "Thou shalt love thy neighbor as thyself."

The words would seem to deserve Akiba's accolade. They do seem to define the ideal standard of conduct and the ultimate goal of society. But perhaps that is why not all of the sages agreed with Akiba: because the words are too ideal, too unrealistic. Is it really possible to love your neighbor as much as you love yourself? How can we love our neighbor when we have not even learned to love our brother? How can God expect us to love everyone when it is such a struggle to love anyone?

Some of the rabbis interpreted the words differently: not "Thou shalt love they neighbor as thyself" but "Thou shalt love thy neighbor who is like thyself." In Hebrew this is almost as plausible, and in terms of human nature it would seem to be more so. God would not ask us to love everyone. Who can love so indiscriminately, so unconditionally? Rather we are expected to love those closest to us, those most like us, in whom we see the nearest reflection of ourselves. Love for all is really an abstraction. No one's arms are long enough to stretch that far. God must really mean that love is meant for those nearby.

Akiba would open the circle of our love as wide as God's. The other sages would close it at the border of kinship. Yet the question is not merely whom we love; it is how we love, whether too wisely, or too well.

I would propose a third interpretation of the ancient commandment. It relies upon the construction of the final Hebrew word. Rabbi Akiba translates it "as yourself"; the other sages, "who is like yourself." However, the Hebrew prefix often has another meaning, "likeness of," referring to a quality or attribute. The most famous example of this usage is found in the creation account of Genesis, where God creates humankind "after His likeness." If this usage is applied to our passage, then it may be understood as: "You shall love your neighbor after your likeness," that is, according to your nature. By this reading the duty to love is not a burden that God imposes but a fulfillment of our own being. The capacity to love is the divine quality already within us. It is as if God were saying, "You shall love your neighbor after your likeness, as I have created you after mine."

It is not that God gives us the commandment to love, but the power to love.

And how great is that power! No stethoscope can detect it, no EKG can trace it, but it is undeniably, invincibly there. I think of the case of Enrique Lopez, nine months old. He is blind, nearly deaf, severely brain damaged. His tiny misshapen body is hooked up to feeding tubes, breathing tubes, electric monitors. According to his doctors and nurses, the only outside stimulus to which Enrique responds is pain, and there is plenty of that. That is, until his mother comes home from work and walks into his hospital room. Immediately Enrique begins waving his arms and legs in excitement. This is the only time he does it. His mother says that he is responding to her voice. The medical staff cannot explain how a child so severely impaired can be so suddenly and electrically aware. Yet to his mother it is no mystery. Her son, in his way, loves her, and she loves her son, with a devotion too fierce for us to understand unless we too have loved a child like Enrique.

She has little money, little education, and little to offer her
son, except her love. But that is no small gift. It is keeping
him alive.

The late Italian Jewish author Primo Levi wrote about a
man he met during his internment in Auschwitz. The man's
name was Lorenzo. He was not a Jew nor an inmate but
an Italian civilian commandeered by the Germans to perform
construction work in the camps. He had no family of his own.
Lorenzo was an expert bricklayer. Levi was an inmate forced
to carry the heavy buckets of poured concrete. He was not
very good at it, in part because he was too small to do it and
in part because, like the other Jews, he was slowly starving
to death.

One day, without explanation, Lorenzo brought Levi a tin
of soup. The danger in this was great: Lorenzo and Levi
belonged to different castes in the Nazi universe. Contact between them was criminal. To help a Jew was to put one's own
life at risk. But this did not deter Lorenzo. Every day for six
months he delivered the soup to the Jewish bucket carrier.
Levi noticed that the soup was never the same: sometimes he
found plum pits, or salami peels, all manner of scraps. He
ate it all, gratefully, because he needed it to survive. Only
later did he find out where the soup came from and why
it contained such motley ingredients: because every evening
Lorenzo would make the rounds of the workers' dormitory,
collecting the residue from their bowls for the starving Jew
who carried the buckets. When this could no longer be done,
he would steal into the camp kitchen in the middle of the
night to scavenge from the cauldrons.

Levi survived the camps and returned to Italy, where he
learned that Lorenzo too had returned to his home. Levi went
to see him so that he could thank him for what he had done,
risking his life to save a stranger's. But here is the sad and
surprising part of the story: he did not find the same man.
Lorenzo, so vigorous, so resourceful, so heroic at Auschwitz,

was now weary, depressed, indifferent to life. He no longer worked as a bricklayer and had turned to drink. With no family of his own, with none to depend on him for soup or for life, with no one to accept his gifts of love, he seemed to have lost his purpose for living. It was then that Levi found out something he had never suspected: all that time in Auschwitz, Lorenzo had fed not only one bucket carrier, but a brigade of them. He had single-handedly saved from starvation a whole labor detail of Jews. In Auschwitz, writes Levi, Lorenzo's life had purpose, but now it was over. He had no one left to save, no one to protect. Soon after their visit Lorenzo died, while Primo Levi, who owed him his life, was left to ponder the power of love.

In a story by Raymond Carver, called "What We Talk About When We Talk About Love," two married couples are sitting around a kitchen table. After a while their conversation turns to the subject of love: what it is, what it isn't, when it's there, when it isn't. Each of them gropes for a description, a definition, but they can't pin it down. Then one of the husbands tells this story.

"There was an old couple who had this car wreck out on the interstate. A drunk driver hit them and they were in very bad shape, and no one was giving them much of a chance to pull through. I was on call that night, and I had just sat down to dinner when the hospital called. Some kid had plowed his dad's pickup into this camper with this old couple in it. They were up in their mid-seventies, this couple. The kid, eighteen or nineteen, was dead on arrival. The old couple, they were just barely alive—multiple fractures, internal injuries, hemorrhaging, the works. And of course their age was two strikes against them.

"By the time I got down there, they had a neurologist and an orthopedist and a couple of surgeons, and we worked on them most of the night. They had these incredible reserves, these two. You see that once in a while. We did everything that could be done, and toward morning we were giving them a fifty-fifty chance, maybe less than that for her.

"So the next morning, here they are, still alive. We moved them into the ICU, where they both kept plugging away at it for two weeks. I dropped in to see them every day. Casts and bandages head to foot, the both of them. You know, you've seen it in the movies, just those little eye-holes and nose-holes and mouth-holes.

"Well, the husband was very depressed for the longest while. Even after we told him that his wife was going to pull through, he was still very depressed. At first we thought it was the trauma of the accident, or the effect of the pain killers. But after more time had passed and the husband was finally strong enough to talk, I leaned over next to the hole for his mouth, and he told me what was the matter. It wasn't the accident. It wasn't the injuries. It was the eye-holes: they weren't big enough for him to see his wife lying in the next bed. I'm telling you, the old man's heart was breaking, not because he might die but because he couldn't turn his head to see his wife."

This is how the Raymond Carver story ends: the two couples are still seated around the table, but now they are quiet, so quiet that they can hear, as if for the first time, the sound of their own hearts beating.

"Thou shalt love, for such have I created thee." If this interpretation of the ancient Hebrew has any merit, it is to remind us that living is empty without love. "Love is strong as death," say the Scriptures, but in truth it is stronger still. No one who has felt its grip upon the heart will doubt it. No one touched by love for just one moment will deny it. In love we are cloaked in a radiance, an astonishment, that surpasses any other experience that we can ever know.

Whose miracle is this? By whose hand is this gift, so unspeakably sweet and powerful, given to us, and given freely? "And that we love!" cried the poet Kenneth Patchen. "Is that not proof of something?"

It is often difficult to think of God as a part of life. We associate Him with the supernatural or with the abstract. If God exists, He is far away, unavailable to ordinary people and aloof from ordinary things. But it is the profound conviction of the Jewish tradition that this is not so. God dwells in every room of the heart. Love is the one door that leads to heaven. And it is when we love that the door opens.

RESPONSIBILITY

WHEN I WAS A CHILD, I first discovered Mr. Nobody. At least that is what my mother called him. It happened one fine afternoon when I was playing baseball in the street. Somehow the ball ended up breaking the neighbor's window. This neighbor wasn't too friendly, so I wasn't about to confess. I ran home and hid in the house. A few minutes later the neighbor came to our door. I heard him tell my mother what happened. She called me into the room.

"Did you throw the baseball?" she asked.

"No," I answered. Technically this was true: I didn't throw the ball, I hit it. In fact, it was the bat that hit the ball.

"Well," my mother said, "you were out there playing. If you didn't break the window, who did?"

This was a tough one. I couldn't think of anything. Finally I said, "Nobody."

"Oh," she said. "I see. Nobody. Mr. Nobody broke the window."

She had turned my lame excuse into a person. This was great! Mr. Nobody: what a concept. A quart of ice cream disappears: Mr. Nobody ate it. The lunch money vanishes: Mr. Nobody spent it. The new jacket is lost: Mr. Nobody took it. I could blame Mr. Nobody for everything.

I wasn't the first to try it. Shifting the blame, evading responsibility, is the most time-honored of human tendencies. It began at the beginning, in the garden of Eden. After Adam eats the forbidden fruit, God confronts him.

"Did you eat of the tree I had forbidden you?"

"The woman that You gave to me," Adam replies, "she gave me the fruit, so I ate it." A classic evasion: Adam defends himself by dividing the blame equally between Eve and God. "The woman was your idea; I didn't ask for her. She gave me the fruit; I didn't ask for it."

Poor Eve: she gets all the blame. But she was a quick study. When God confronts her, she is ready. "It wasn't me," she explains. "It was the serpent. He beguiled me. That's why I did it." As one commentator has observed, it is too bad that the conversation between God and the serpent is not reported. It would have been interesting to hear the serpent's excuse.

Laying the blame upon others for the wrongs that we commit is a chronic human failing. It is also understandable. Accountability is a painful business. It requires us to confront ourselves, in the depths of our conscience, with our deeds; to judge ourselves, unsparingly, for our failures; and to submit ourselves, without evasion, to the consequences. This kind of reckoning is called by the rabbis *heshbon ha-nefesh,* an inventory of the soul. The premise is that we are held to account by our Creator: credited for our virtues, culpable for our faults, and liable for our lives before the Judge of all the living. In the words of the Jewish prayer book, "He records and recounts. He remembers all that we have forgotten. He opens the book of our days, and what is written there proclaims itself, for it bears the signature of every living being." Mr. Nobody does not appear in this book. When Adam and Eve transgressed, they hid from God in the garden. But He found them.

Even so, are we always responsible? Is there never a justification or extenuation that would excuse our transgressions? None of us is a completely free agent. All of us are part of a greater fabric; the threads are interwoven. Some compromises cannot be avoided, and some obstacles cannot be overcome. "The fate of all things is beyond our control," the Jewish sages concede. But with typical astringency they add: "Even so, our deeds are our own." We are rarely mere victims of circumstance, even if it can be convenient, and expedient, to think so.

The journalist John Taylor has discussed the growing trend in American society for people of all creeds, colors, and incomes, the guilty as well as the innocent, to ascribe to themselves the status of victims: to find someone or something to blame for whatever is wrong with their lives. Cigarette smokers blame their habit on the tobacco companies. Fearful airline passengers blame their fear on the airlines. People who watch too much television blame the television. Credible legal complaints are giving way to the incredible. A man who injured himself in a refrigerator race—that is where competitors strap refrigerators to their backs and see who can run the fastest—sued the manufacturers of the refrigerator. He claimed that they should have warned him not to run with a refrigerator on his back!

As Taylor points out, a greater focus on the victim has brought overdue justice to the truly victimized. The plight of battered women and the pain of abused children are now more likely to be addressed. Victims of violent crimes, often forgotten once the crime is committed, are now treated with greater consideration. But what began as well-intentioned redress has led to a kind of victimization inflation. In the rush to establish ever more categories of victims, Taylor argues, the ethic of individual responsibility is disappearing.

A commonplace today is the legal defense of mental disease, disorder, or diminished capacity. The pioneer claim of this kind, authorized a decade ago by the American Psychiatric Association's Diagnostic and Statistical Manual, is PTSD, post-traumatic stress disorder. Since then various subcategories have sought similar recognition: victimization disorder; depression-suicide syndrome; oppression artifact disorder. Trauma syndromes may well be helpful as models of therapeutic treatment, and they may lend legitimate support to pleas of self-defense or temporary insanity. But the danger, now more and more often encountered, is when the syndrome or disorder becomes a blanket excuse. Addictions, too, are now defined as diseases in ever expanding profusion: gambling, drinking, shopping, jogging, eating too much, eating too little. However useful these may be as categories of treatment, they also have the effect of excusing or even justifying injurious conduct, convincing us that our own behavior is beyond our control.

A brave new world of evasion may not be far off. Biochemical research is now said to suggest a new model of human volition that attributes, or more accurately, reduces, human behavior to chemical reactions. It has been discovered, for example, that certain males have an extra Y chromosome, linked by some researchers to antisocial behavior. This has led to a legal debate about the possibility of an "XYY chromosome defense." If one follows this kind of deduction to its logical conclusion, what becomes of free will? What happens when the notion of right or wrong is superseded by biochemicals?

Nor is the retreat from responsibility confined to the courtrooms. Consider the typical language of political discourse today, especially when it is on the defensive. The columnist William Safire has noted the growing preference for the tense of "past exonerative," viz., "Mistakes were made," somehow leaving oneself out of the sentence; or "New taxes have been imposed," suggesting that how this happened is a mystery. The actor is divorced from the act. While this kind of linguistic evasion may seem innocuous, it can be lethal. In Nazi Germany, to take the most heinous example, government edicts were purposely crafted to deflect accountability. As the late historian Lucy Dawidowicz has shown, sentences were intentionally composed with passive constructions and intransitive verbs: "Prompt Aryanization is to be sought.... The handling of the problem will meet with certain difficulties. . . . " Personal responsibility is disclaimed. The structure and syntax of this language convey the sense that things happen as a consequence of vast impersonal forces without visible agents. That is what the Nazis wanted people to think. It helps to explain why, at the Nuremberg trials, no S.S. officer seemed to have any idea how those gas chambers got there, or how so many Jews got locked inside.

In the Jewish morning prayers, there is a benediction, "Praised art Thou, O Lord our God, who has not made me a slave." The commentators explain that this is not an expression of relief as much as an avowal of responsibility. A slave cannot be held accountable for deeds performed under the lash of servitude. But a free person is liable for what he or she does. A free person is accountable before God. This is what gives our deeds—and our lives—their meaning.

The book of life is open before Him. But the handwriting is not His. Each of us signs our own name. We write the stories of our lives. Only the ledger is God's; it is we who make the entries, day by day, until the ink runs out. It is we who hold each moment in our hands, and we who choose whether to hallow or to profane it. Adam and Eve fled from God. But they could not flee from responsibility before Him. Only when they accepted the consequences of their deeds were they ready to leave the garden of their childhood behind. Only then were they ready to grow up and go forth in all their human dignity.

Here is the end of my childhood incident with the baseball and the broken window:

"So," my mother said, "where is this Mr. Nobody?"

"He's invisible," I said. "You can't see him."

She leaned down and looked me straight in the eye and said: "Oh yes I can."

GOODNESS

IN ITS POETIC WAY, the book of Genesis describes the work of creation: the firmament and the stars, all that grows and all that breathes. Each day of divine labor closes with a brief verdict: "And it was good." This judgment is no surprise: it is an axiom of Judaism that God is good, as is everything He says or does. "The law of the Lord is perfect," says the Psalmist, "His testimony is sure, His precepts are right, His judgments are true." In the daily Jewish prayers, God is called goodness itself. If all this is so, the Jewish sages ask, why does the Torah go to such lengths to state the obvious? Of course the creation is good. Whey does the Torah underline this when it need not be said at all?

A sixteenth-century rabbi called Sforno has advanced this theory: the Torah is not merely stating the obvious. It is saying something else entirely: not about the quality of God's work, but its purpose; not His skill at creating things, but His motive for doing so. When the Torah says, "And it was good," Sforno writes, the Torah means, "It was for the sake of good." God called the universe out of nothing so that He might infuse it with His goodness. He created us in His image so that, like Him, we might do good. Our lives are meant to be opportunities for holiness, for deeds of tenderness, compassion, and generosity. God created us so that, by every act of goodness, we might come to know Him, and that He might live within us.

To be sure, this definition of the word "good" is an exalted

113

one, and not the most popular these days. The word "good"
has come to mean something else: not virtue, but technique;
not rectitude, but aptitude. When we ask someone for the
name of a "good" attorney, we mean someone expert, if not
cunning or even ruthless. When my son tells me that the boy
up the block is "good," he is not talking about the boy's conduct but about his skill on a skateboard. More and more, to
be good means to be good *at* something, no matter what it is.
I recall a recent movie about an assassin, a "hit man," trailed
by two police detectives. In the course of their investigation,
they marvel at the murderer's technique and precision. In one
scene, they find that a victim has been shot to death from a
distant rooftop. The bullet hole is right between the eyes. The
two detectives recognize the hit man's work. "Wow," one says
to the other in a tone of awe, "this guy is *good.*"

The adulteration of a word, were it only that, is not so
serious. But when good refers only to proficiency, when success counts for more than virtue, when performance counts
for more than anything, then the divine purpose of creation
is thwarted. Sforno would say that, by eviscerating the word
"good" of its exalted ambition, we are driving God out of
our hearts.

And God is not our only victim. Ask our children. Our
stress on success, on being good *at,* starts early these days.
They must sign up for the proper infant program so that they
can enroll in a quality preschool which will qualify them for
learning-intensive kindergarten. By the time they are adolescents, such children are expected to be performance machines.
But the incessant pressure takes its toll. American society today has the highest rate of child suicide ever recorded. Among
fifteen- to nineteen-year-olds, only car accidents take more
lives than suicide, and many of those are suspected suicides.
Among all the reasons for this, psychologists identify one con-
sistent factor: a feeling of emptiness. Adolescents grope for
words to describe the void in their lives, the want of some-

thing to live for, to stand for. It is not hard to see how this void opens. If you are no good at competing, no good at succeeding, you begin to think that you are no good, period. When life is reduced to a contest, Harold Kushner has written, there will always be losers, and even the winners will wonder what it is they have won.

It is not that we don't love our children. On the contrary, most of us are earnestly, extravagantly devoted to them. We want them to have more than we have, to be more than we are. But somewhere along the line we have lost the Torah's perspective. We have altered the measure of our children's success. We have taught them to revere only what they can hold in their hands, as if the intangible were a swindle. If there is no more to making a life than making a living, the Torah becomes irrelevant. If we value only what is useful for getting things done, then every other way of thinking seems like a foolish waste of time. How often do we ask our children, "What doth the Lord require of thee?" We are too busy asking, "What doth Harvard require of thee? What doth Stanford require of thee?"

Later on in the book of Genesis, the time arrives for the patriarch Jacob (also called Israel) to die. He summons his son Joseph to hear his last request: "Please do not bury me in Egypt. Take me up from here and let me lie down with my fathers in their burial place." Joseph replies, "I will do as you wish." Israel says, "Swear to me," and Joseph swears to him. Then, the Torah says, "Israel bowed down at the head of the bed."

The Jewish sages were perplexed by this last sentence. Why would Jacob suddenly bow down? The Torah commands that the child should honor the father, but here the father honors the child. The roles are reversed: it should be Joseph, out of respect for his father's last wish, who does the bowing; instead it is Jacob, on his own death bed, who bows to his son.

An obvious explanation is that Jacob bowed down to

Joseph because his son was the viceroy of Egypt. Jacob was Joseph's father, but he was also his subject. However, an ancient midrash insists otherwise. Jacob was not really bowing to Joseph, the midrash says, but to God. He was praying. He was giving thanks to God that his son Joseph was a good son. Jacob rejoiced not because Joseph was famous and successful but because even so, and more important, he was a righteous man and a loving son.

If Sforno is right, here is what we can learn from the divine verdict of creation: more important than being good at something is being good to someone. To be kind and decent and true is why we are here and what we are meant to do. When the divine ledger is opened, the only entries that matter are the good we have done and the love we have known. Everything else, in Shakespeare's phrase, is sound and fury, signifying nothing. If we can teach this to our children, then perhaps, like Jacob, someday we too will be privileged to bow at the head of the bed and thank God that our lives were not in vain.

FORGIVENESS

PRAYER IS NOT the original form of Jewish worship. Before there were rabbis, there were priests; before there was a temple, there was a tabernacle; before there was an ark, there was an altar. The ancient way of worship was to burn offerings within a sacred shrine. The fire that consumed the offering was a symbol of purification and holiness. When the high priest made atonement for Israel's sins, he approached the altar. But before he could kindle the flame, the Torah prescribes one critical task: the ashes had to be removed. Why was this so important? Because, the sages explain, the altar fire must be bright, and the flame burns brighter when there are no ashes beneath.

Were the Torah's meaning confined to the archaic, this detail would be of little interest. But the Jewish way is to peer beneath the antique surface to search out the deeper metaphor. The flame may be understood as our own life, and the ashes as life's debris, the residue of the past. For the flame to burn brightly, the ashes must be cleared away. Life must forge ahead. It may acknowledge its debt to the past, but it cannot be its prisoner. The old failures and hurts, the lingering grudges and broken ambitions, can haunt our days and darken our nights. The flame sputters from all the ashes of anger and regret. It is better, the rabbis suggest, to sweep away the ashes and cleanse the altar, so that the flame can burn bright and free. Instead of crippling ourselves with remorse, we release ourselves to the future.

A simple message, perhaps, but not so easily learned. Some time ago I was told of a middle-aged man who used to be a soccer player. Every Sunday this man did the same thing. He went to the park by himself and kicked his soccer ball. He would always do it just this way: he would begin about fifty feet in front of the goal. First he would maneuver the ball to the right, then to the left, then to the right again, until he was directly in front of the goal. Then he would tap the ball into the net with his right instep, and turn around, and raise his hand in the air. Again and again he would do this, like a figurine on a Dresden clock.

Watching this punishing routine of repetitions, one might have thought that the man was practicing for a big game. But it turns out that the big game was twenty years before, on a grassy field in Liverpool, England. The man was punishing himself, all right, but for something that had happened long ago. "It was the championship game," he recalled, "and there was only a minute left. All of a sudden I had the ball, and there was no defender in front of me. I faked to the right, then to the left, then to the right again. The goalie was out of position. All I had to do was tap the ball into the net, and we win. But I tried to be fancy. I kicked it too hard. The ball sailed off to the right, out of bounds. We lost the game and the championship."

Then, having rehearsed once again this moment of failure, having opened once again the old wound, having heaped up still higher the burned-out ashes of regret, the man returned to his ritual. "Here's the way I should have done it," he said, and he did the whole thing all over again. Right, left, right, kick. Hand in the air.

All the other gifts of forgiveness, whether from those we have wronged or from God Himself, mean little if we cannot learn to forgive ourselves. When we persist in reliving the old defeats, they lodge in our hearts like rust. To torture ourselves with the memory of failure is to corrode the spirit, to weaken the altar flame. As Lewis Smedes has written, nothing we attempt is free of error. Nothing we achieve is ever faultless. To forgive ourselves is to let what was, go. It is to free ourselves from the tyranny of bitterness. It is to settle for the title of human.

If we can do that, perhaps then we can begin to forgive each other. This is harder still, as the great sage Maimonides recognized long ago. For those of our deeds that hurt others, he writes, we must allay the anger of the injured parties, placate them, and make peace with them. If after three entreaties they still refuse to forgive us, then we have fulfilled our duty. But that is not all: now they become the guilty ones, for now they are the ones to inflict injury. They have refused to be reconciled, refused to forgive, and this too is a sin.

The bitterest tears we shed are for the words of love left unsaid, the deeds left undone, the forgiveness foregone. Walter Wangerin has related a story of his early years of marriage. He and his wife would fight all the time. The fights were one-sided: he talked, she didn't; she cried, he didn't. He would ask her why she was crying, as if he didn't know; she would cry even harder, as if he didn't care. He knew what she was up to: tears were her strategy to make him feel guilty. So he would do her one better: he would make her feel even guiltier. Jamming his arms into his overcoat, he would bolt down the stairs of their little apartment, slam the door, and storm out into the cold night, there to roam the streets for hours on end, confident that she was left feeling miserable and worried sick.

These fights went on, infrequently, then more frequently, until one night, after the usual script of undeserved accusations and tears, the jamming on of the overcoat and the storming down the stairs, something unexpected happened: when he, in his self-righteous anger, slammed the front door, his coat got caught. Angrier by the moment, he searched his pockets for the key to unlock the door, but he had forgotten it. Here he was, out in the cold, stuck in the door, with two alternatives: either to shed the coat and walk around for hours without it, in which case he would freeze, or to ring the doorbell, which after ten minutes of debate, he did.

His wife came down the stairs and peered out at him, his face red and his coat stuck in the door. When she opened it she was laughing, laughing so hard that the tears began to stream down her face and she had to put her hand on his shoulder to hold herself up.

He could have smiled too, at least a little bit. He could even have joined in the laughter, seeing how ridiculous he looked, knowing that their fight was now forgotten and that their love for each other was more important than their arguments. He could have realized that the coat in the door was a gift of reconciliation between wife and husband, that to laugh is to forgive and forget and start over.

But he did not laugh. He did not even smile. Too proud, too embarrassed by his predicament, too determined to punish her still, he batted her hand from his shoulder and stalked off, more grimly than before. Pride served, anger abetted, forgiveness foregone.

"Learn from me," Wangerin concludes, "you husbands and wives, you children and parents. Learn, all of you who suffer fallings-out with one another, who prefer to lick your wounds in proud isolation. It is God who prepares the way of reconciliation, even by so small a thing as a coat in a door."

What distinguishes God from us, the Jewish tradition teaches, is that He is always ready to forgive. Of the two fundamental divine attributes, justice and mercy, it is mercy that prevails. Were it not so, the rabbis teach, the earth could not stand for a moment. The gates of forgiveness are open wide, and all may enter. So anxious is God to forgive us, taught the prophet Isaiah, that He answers us before we call; He hears us before we speak.

To forgive is to acknowledge that love is a risk, but a risk worth taking; that pain is not always an injustice but the way of learning that love must travel. The past is irretrievable. We must forgive it the pain it has brought us, even as we thank it for the joy we have known. To squint vainly backward into the darkness is to waste what little light we have. There is too little time in this life to squander it on sorrow. In recalling the ancient rite of sacrifice, the rabbis have taught us well: the beauty of the altar is found in the flame, not in the ashes.

OLD AGE

A RABBI ONCE TOLD ME about an old man in failing health who lived by himself in a rundown section of the Bronx. The rabbi went to visit him. In the threadbare apartment the old man had set a table between two chairs. On the table were two glasses of tea and a few letters. After they had poured the tea, the old man showed the rabbi the letters. They were from the old man's son. His son, said the old man, was a wonderful son with a wonderful family. They sent him money each month to pay the rent. Once a year, without fail, they all came to visit him there in the Bronx. The rabbi thought: How good to hear of such a devoted son. As the old man cleared the glasses away, the rabbi glanced at the letters on the table. Only then did he see that the son's return address was quite close by, on Long Island.

Such sorrows may not be typical, but they are not unique either. They are the inevitable by-product of a society that sets the elderly aside, that dreads the advance of old age. Ours is a culture where what is young is what is beautiful, where it is rude to ask a person's age, where the impress of years is hidden beneath layers of make-up and mascara. One need only notice the ads in the magazines or the actors in the movies to realize that youth is our god; being young is divine. We spend more time concealing the "disease" of age than healing disease itself. There are not as many patients in the hospitals as there are in the beauty parlors.

The comedian Woody Allen once was asked what he would

like people to say about him a hundred years from now. He answered: "I hope they will say, 'He looks good for his age.' " That is how is it with us: old age is something we are anxious to attain, until we attain it. Then the victory becomes a defeat, the privilege a punishment. In the convalescent homes or the lonely apartments, one does not sense the eminence of age, the harvest of long experience. More often one sees the fearful and the forgotten, clinging to life and to the hope of someone's affection.

As Abraham Joshua Heschel has written, what we owe the old is esteem, but all they ask is consideration, attention, not to be discarded or forgotten. What they deserve is preference, yet we do not even grant them equality. Care for the aged is often regarded as an act of charity rather than a matter of justice. In some ancient cultures it was the practice to abandon the very old in the wilderness, where they were left to die. Nowadays an old person can be placed in a luxury hotel and left to die.

One of the most touching stories in the Torah concerns the patriarch Joseph and his reunification with his family after long years apart. Now risen to great wealth and power in Egypt, Joseph is not recognized at first by the estranged brothers who once abandoned him. At last he reveals his true identity: "I am Joseph." His next words: "Is my father still alive?" Joseph's very first concern is the welfare of his aged father, Jacob, whom he has not forgotten even after all the years of separation. Next Joseph brings Jacob to Egypt and provides for his every material need. This act of filial devotion deserves our admiration. Yet according to the medieval commentator Sforno, Joseph had a still more important motive. Why did he say to his brothers, "Bring my father here"? Sforno explains: "So that Jacob could rejoice to *see* his son." It was not enough for Joseph to make his aged father comfortable. He wanted to make him happy, and he understood that what was most precious to the father was not the son's wealth but the son's nearness.

Jewish tradition views mother and father as partners with God in our creation. In the Ten Commandments, the God of Israel does not proclaim: "Honor Me, revere Me." Rather He enjoins us to honor our parents, not only for their sake, but for His. Honor shown to them is shown to God, for it acknowledges His claim as well. By professing our debt to our creators, we admit that we are not the source of our own being, that we owe our existence to others. Our elders are the thread on which our own lives are strung. They are the branch of which we are the blossom. Like the acorn that has fallen from the oak, we may feel that we are self-sufficient. But the source of our life is still in the oak that formed us. The countenance of the oak is encoded in the acorn's heart. In the same way, who and what we are did not begin with us. We are the vessels of a life we did not make, that has no price, that is a gift. Our elders were the first ones to hold us. They were the ones who loved us long before we loved them.

There are things about our parents and grandparents that we think we know. But there are other things, divine things, that we never know: the backbreaking hours of work to provide for us; the glow of pride in their eyes when they gazed at us; the things they did without because of us; the blanket to cover our chests at night; the gentle hand on a fevered brow; the stricken look when we were sad or hurt...in a thousand ways was love conveyed.

How can we neglect them? How can we be so ungrateful?

"Do not cast me off in the time of old age," cries the Psalmist. "When my strength is spent, do not forsake me." The greatest tragedy of the aged is not when their health fails them but when we fail them; when we shrink from them; when we leave them to the imaginary visitors they dream of, or to the sons and daughters they never see.

Since hearing the story of the old man in the Bronx, I have had many occasions to think of him. Some would consider him lucky to have a son who sends him money. Yet I picture him proudly displaying his son's letters and silently crying, "Where can he be?" Where can they be, the families of these frail and dying old people, perishing more from lack of love than from lack of oxygen?

Some cemeteries and mausoleums now offer a new service. For a fee they will provide what they call "perpetual care," fresh flowers for the grave or crypt every week of the year. It is a thoughtful gesture. But it is also a belated one. The most fragrant flowers are the ones we give to the living.

GOD'S IMAGE

RICHARD BAUSCH has written a story that I seem unable to forget. It is about a little girl name Brenda. She is in the fifth grade. Her father left her mother, and then her mother died in a car accident, so she lives with her grandfather. She is a good student at school, but she is ungainly and bulky. In order to lose weight, she has set for herself a program of exercise and dieting. This is in preparation for a PTA meeting during which the children of the fifth grade will perform a gymnastics demonstration. There will be a vaulting horse and a little trampoline. All of the children are supposed to propel themselves over the horse to the other side. But no matter how hard she tries, Brenda is the only one in the class who can't do it.

So every morning, very early, she goes out to the backyard for her training regimen, trying breathlessly to jump rope or turn somersaults. Her grandfather watches her earnest efforts from the window. He knows how the other children tease her. His heart aches for her. But what can he do?

On the morning of the PTA meeting, Brenda is out in the yard extra early, but when she comes in for breakfast—orange juice only, because of her diet—she is discouraged. "I guess I'm not going to make it over the vaulting horse after all," she says to her grandfather.

"Sure you will," he says.

"But what if I don't?"

"Honey, sometimes people just aren't good at these

126

things," her grandfather says. "Lots of people never do anything like this."

"I'm the only one I know," Brenda says dejectedly. Her grandfather thinks of the cruel pressure of this gymnastics exercise, where all of the children and all of the parents will be watching; what it would feel like being the only one to fail. He doesn't know what to say to her.

That night the PTA meeting is crowded with parents and children. The gymnastics demonstration begins. Each child vaults over the horse. At last it is Brenda's turn. As she steadies herself to run and jump, her grandfather sees her looking for his face in the crowd. He lifts his hand to wave, feeling as though his heart will break . . . and here the story ends.

We are not told whether Brenda makes it over the vaulting horse or not. The story is not about whether she makes it, but why it is so important to her, and how the one person who loves her cannot help her. Here is this little girl, lonely, awkward, and orphaned, who has come to believe that her worth as a person depends upon how high she can jump.

Stories like this are told again and again. Recently the wire services reported a new self-help group in southern California for dropouts from all the other self-help groups. This one is called Failures Anonymous. The local newspaper reported as follows: "Take a moment to meet the people who have surrendered to the realization that their lives have amounted to one big nothing. Meet Herb, Allen, Keith, and Mary: self-admitted zeroes. For them, Failures Anonymous is the last stand." The article goes on to describe a typical group meeting. Mary is the first to speak. "Hello, everyone," she says. "My name is Mary, and I'm a failure." It seems that Mary's husband died five years before, and now she doesn't know what to do with herself. "After he died," she says, "I tried to go back to school, but I couldn't do it. I can't keep a job. I can't do anything," she concludes, her eyes beginning to brim with tears. The other failures say nothing to comfort her; Failures Anonymous does not work that way. Instead you are supposed to say something good about yourself. Keith, another failure, cannot think of anything. He is unemployed, his wife divorced him, he is out of money. "Well," he sighs at last, "yesterday I did my laundry." That is the only good thing about himself that he can name.

This story, in all of its versions, rests on a premise that many people today seem to share: that the worth of a human being is conditional. If I jump over the vaulting horse, then I will be loved; if I am successful, then my life will count. Many of us think of ourselves this way. We make esteem for ourselves contingent upon the esteem of others. We reduce our lives to a contest for their acclaim. We act as if our final value is something that other people confer. If I don't matter to them, I don't matter. If they say I am a failure, if they say I am clumsy, or slow, or ugly, then that is exactly what I am.

A few years ago a book appeared about a young woman in Philadelphia born with neurofibromatosis, the disorder known as Elephant Man's disease. It disfigures the body, not the soul. (It takes other people to do that.) When this young woman, as a child, would board the school bus, the other children would taunt her: "Here comes the monster, here comes the monster." After a while she found a way to get them to stop: she would say it herself. Every time she got on the bus, she would announce her arrival: "Here comes the monster, here comes the monster." Their name for her became her name for herself.

Judaism has another name for her, and for every one of us. It is called, in Hebrew, *tselem elohim*, the image of God. It is a name that is not learned, or earned, or contrived. It is given by God, not by the children on the school bus. It means that the worth of a human being is unconditional. It does not lie in the measure of acclaim or success, beauty or intellect. Human worth is found in relation to God. A person has value because he or she has value to God. When the Torah says that we are formed in the divine image, it means that each of us has supreme value. Each of us is a divine disclosure, a vessel of holiness. Our minds may be limited, our will may be weak, yet nothing can deprive us of our ultimate dignity. It was out of love that God gave us life. He filled our lungs with His own breath. The ancient rabbis taught: How greatly God must have loved us to create us; yet even greater love did He show by telling us He created us.

But do we know who we are, for whom we stand? Do we behold our own splendor? There is a legend about a king who owned a magnificent peacock. One day he decided to sew up the peacock's head inside a sack, so there would be nothing to distract from the beauty of the tail. The bird, meanwhile, forgot what it looked like. It came to assume that all existence was encompassed by the sack. Its own beauty was beyond its comprehension. Is it not also so with us? Are we not, in Heschel's phrase, messengers who have forgotten the message?

I imagine that little girl, Brenda, anxiously waiting her turn to jump over the vaulting horse, searching desperately for her grandfather's face in the crowd, for some assurance of love. I wish someone in the story would say to her: Whether or not you jump over the horse, whether or not you are clumsy or chubby, whether or not you have parents to love you—you are a child of God, His own treasure, the light of His eyes. And because you bear His image, you are someone infinitely precious, exquisite, and unrepeatable. There will never be anyone else, ever, exactly like you. The vaulting horse doesn't matter; *you* matter.

It has been taught: When God created human beings, the angels were envious. Having heard that these beings were formed in God's likeness, they conspired to hide the divine image from them. One of the angels wanted to hide it in the depths of the ocean. Another proposed to bury it on the highest mountain. But the shrewdest of all the angels had a better idea: "Let us hide the divine image in their own hearts. That is the last place they will look for it."

Defects

O F ALL THE ANCIENT ISRAELITES, only the priests were considered holy by birth. They alone were permitted to perform the divine service. They alone were empowered to purge impurity and heal disease. They alone blessed the people in the name of God. But in order to maintain their holiness, as it was then defined, the priesthood was severely restricted. Special requirements were imposed concerning marriage, the consumption of food, and contact with the dead. Even those who qualified in every other respect were excluded from the altar unless they were free of any blemish or physical defect.

"The Lord spoke to Moses saying: No priest who is blemished shall make an offering to God ... neither the blind, the lame, the halt, the hunchback, the dwarf, nor one who is maimed, or injured, or diseased. No priest with such a defect is permitted to approach the altar."

Granting the antiquity of this passage and acknowledging the strict requirements of the Israelite priesthood, I still find these verses puzzling. Does Judaism not teach divine compassion and human equality? Have we not learned from the rabbis that holiness lies deeper than the skin? Is it a disgrace to be blind or lame? Can the Torah really mean that such defects make us less acceptable to God?

Nor is there much comfort in the pages of the Talmud, where these strictures are elaborated. There it is argued that a priest should also be disqualified if his head is misshapen, if he is bald, if his teeth are missing, if his eyes are too weak, if his feet are too wide, if his skin is too black or too white or too red. Nowhere in the Talmud, to my knowledge, is there any objection to the notion that a priest is disqualified by physical defect. In fact, Samson Raphael Hirsch, renowned for reinterpreting ancient ideas, defends this one: "It is not the afflicted and the infirm, not the disfigured and crippled, for whom the Jewish altar is erected. . . . It is life in its completeness, in its freshness and strength. . . . It demands the surrender of the whole human being. . . . That is why it must be perfect, complete men who perform the offerings in the Sanctuary." From my point of view, this interpretation does not help, for it still suggests that physical flaws or impairments reduce one's stature before God.

Maimonides offers another explanation. The reason that the priest is disqualified by physical defects, he explains, is not because God disapproves of them, but because we do. For instance, when the priest stands before the congregation to invoke the priestly blessing, any physical anomaly of his would be likely to distract them. They would tend to stare at a missing finger, a disfigured eye, or discolored skin. This would have the effect of diverting their attention from the worship of God. By this interpretation, the prohibition of priestly defects is not a divine preference but a divine concession to human nature. We tend to notice what is flawed; in our eyes, defects are unbecoming. But not in the eyes of God.

With all due reverence, I would go even further than Maimonides. I would argue that it is our defects, not our perfection, that God requires; our limitations, not our faultless grace. For it is by these, our impairments, that God instructs us, that our defects may teach us what our blessings cannot.

For proof I turn first to the example of Jacob, the first to be called Israel. So great has been his influence and so deep his impress that his name has been assumed by all the generations of his descendants. But to look at Jacob's early life, one might wonder how this happened. While his grandfather Abraham was the most righteous of men, and his father, Isaac, the most gentle, Jacob was neither of these. He had a twin brother, Esau, who as the firstborn was lawfully entitled to inherit Isaac's legacy. But Jacob wanted this birthright for himself, and by extortion he forced Esau to relinquish it. Later on, Isaac announced his wish to bestow his blessing upon Esau. This time Jacob, with his mother's collaboration, contrived by disguise and deceit to steal his brother's blessing. To this point, Jacob appears to be a man without a conscience. He would not give a bowl of soup to his own brother without exacting a price.

Then something happens to change Jacob forever. He finds himself on the bank of a river. He is tired and frightened and alone. For years he had been running from Esau, whom he had so grievously wronged. But now Esau was waiting for him with four hundred armed men. The moment of reckoning was at hand. Having sent his household ahead of him, Jacob remained by himself in the darkness. Then someone—perhaps an angel, though the Hebrew is ambiguous—someone wrestled with Jacob until the dawn. Jacob was the stronger, and he won the angel's blessing. But he did not emerge unscathed. In the course of the struggle, he injured his hip. When the sun rose, Jacob found that he could not walk without limping. Some commentators say that the injury healed, but others suggest that the limp was permanent. Had Jacob been a priest, he would no longer have been allowed to approach the altar, for he was now among the lame and the halt.

Yet it is by our impairments that God instructs us. Not only was Jacob's outward bearing changed by his injury; he was inwardly transformed. As several commentators observe, Jacob's limp had the effect of deepening his empathy and compassion. Once eager to exploit his vulnerable brother, he was now vulnerable himself. As he limped to his meeting with Esau, the old swagger was gone. Were he to hurt or deceive his brother now, he would not be nimble enough to run away, as he had before. The man who was so agile had now become more fragile. Jacob had often hurt others without feeling it; now he felt it with every step. No longer could he remain unmoved by his brother's pain. What a birthright and a blessing could not teach him, Jacob learned from a limp.

There is a biblical forebear of still greater distinction who was burdened by a still greater deficit. He is the most powerful figure in all the Hebrew Bible, commanding our admiration and even our awe. He was the master of all the prophets, the only mortal ever to behold God face to face. His name was Moses.

One might think that a man of such awesome stature would be the first to qualify for the priestly service. Surely Moses, of all men, was without flaw or defect. But this is not so. Moses lived with a severe disability, particularly for a prophet charged to proclaim the word of God. For Moses, as the Torah mentions more than once, was slow of speech and slow of tongue. One commentator interprets this to mean that he could not pronounce words distinctly; another suggests that he stuttered. Either way, his speech defect must have been serious: God Himself acknowledges the need for a surrogate to speak for him. "I set you in God's stead to Pharaoh," He says to Moses, "but Aaron your brother shall be your prophet. You shall repeat all that I command you, but your brother Aaron will speak to Pharaoh." Imagine this: a prophet with a speech impairment, proclaiming a message he cannot even pronounce. It seems almost perverse. Where is the divine wisdom in this? Why, as Moses himself asks of God, would You choose a man like me?

Because Moses, like Jacob, had something to learn from his disability. One called to speak in the name of God might easily forget that he is merely a man. One at whose word the Nile turns to blood might easily conclude that it is his own doing. But Moses could hardly speak for himself, let alone for God.

Every time he opened his mouth, his struggling tongue would remind him of his imperfect humanity. Perhaps God singled out Moses just because of his speech defect, for it assured his humility. Only the humblest of men could be trusted with the utmost of powers. Only a man with no gift for speech would never mistake God's voice for his own.

Jacob and Moses, the two towering pillars of ancient Jewish faith, each lived with a disability. One limped and one stuttered. One could hardly walk and one could hardly talk. Neither of them could have approached the holy altar, where only the flawless may stand. Yet each of them came even nearer to God. Both Jacob and Moses ascended to the summit of the spirit, not despite their limitations but because of them. It was their defects that recommended them to God, and their weakness that taught them strength.

Of course, we are neither Jacob nor Moses. Our lives are rarely inspiring or heroic. Yet we too have defects, limitations, and obstacles to overcome. If it is not a limp or a stutter, then it is a disease or an illness, a cataract or a tumor, a weak heart or an aching one. It is a bereavement or a rejection, a heavy burden or a silent sorrow. We are not as flawless as the ancient priests, nor are we as brilliant, as fortunate, or as beautiful as we would like to be. Maybe we have been hurt by life in such a way that it is not the body but the soul that limps from day to day.

Yet if we can learn from the example of those who have struggled, who have persevered and overcome, then we too may find a strength we never suspected. "Broken vessels are scorned by people," says an ancient midrash, "but God uses them." It was a limp, not an angel, that taught Jacob compassion; a stutter, not a speech, that taught Moses to be humble. Our defects can teach us what our blessings cannot.

When the wind strips the leaves from the branches, the tree may not be as strong or as lovely to behold. But only then, when the branches are bare, can we see all the way into the forest.

Miracles

Walt Whitman once wrote that

> every hour of the light and dark is a miracle.
> Every cubic inch of space is a miracle.

This is the poetic definition of the miraculous: the beauty that we fail to notice, the hours that we take for granted, the wonders of the commonplace. This kind of miracle is a natural rather than a supernatural event, perennial rather than peculiar; comprising, rather than transcending, the order of things. If we think of the miraculous at all in our days, most of us will think in Whitman's terms, the ones poets can express and science can explain.

The Torah, in contrast, describes miracles of a different magnitude, beyond the reach of poetry or proof. "As Pharaoh drew near, the Israelites saw the Egyptians advancing upon them. They were greatly frightened, and they cried out to the Lord.... The Lord said to Moses: Let the Egyptians know that I am the Lord.... Then Moses held out his arm over the sea, and the Lord drove back the sea with a strong east wind all that night and turned the sea into dry ground. The waters were divided...and the Israelites marched through the sea on dry ground, the waters forming a wall for them on either side. Thus the Lord delivered Israel that day from the Egyptians.... And when Israel saw the wondrous power which the Lord had wielded, the people feared the Lord. They had faith in the Lord and in his servant Moses."

Here is the supernatural miracle par excellence, an amaz-
ing case of divine intervention, contravening the law of nature
and the rule of reason. Of course, those who would reduce
every phenomenon to the verifiable have sought to attribute
this event to a natural, not a supernatural force: an earthquake, a tidal wave, or even a solar disturbance. But the
ancients thought otherwise. They were not as troubled as we
are by the distance between the possible and the impossible. It
was their conviction that, for God, no such distinction exists.
They did not question His ability to do anything. He who
created the world could certainly divide the sea. The miracle
was the proof of His power. Notice that the proof was not
lost on the Israelites: "They saw the power that the Lord had
wielded, and they had faith in the Lord." They were believers.
It was the miracle that created the faith.

By the time of the ancient rabbis, it was already recognized
that miracles on this scale could no longer be expected. In the
days of the Second Temple, rabbinic sources tell us that only
minor miracles were still occurring: in Jerusalem, scorpions
lost their sting; in the Temple, the altar fire never went out;
no matter how many pilgrims crowded the Temple courtyard,
there was always room to bow. This catalogue of the miraculous hardly compares with the Torah's. It would seem that even
the rabbis, for all their faith, were not so sure about miracles.

Neither are we. Few of us today truly believe that a woman
turned into a pillar of salt, or that a shepherd's staff turned
into a snake, or that a donkey opened its mouth and spoke.
The Torah reports each of these miracles, but the modern
mind objects. If such miracles create faith, then we are not
believers. These stories may have lessons to teach, but truth
is not one of them.

But there is another way to think about miracles, another
way to recognize them, to appreciate the power and the presence of God. I am thinking of a story told many years ago by
Rabbi Isaac Luria.

Once there were two poor Jews, simple men of greater faith than learning. One of them was the baker in the town; the other was the caretaker of the synagogue. One Sabbath day the baker heard the rabbi say that in the days of the Temple in Jerusalem, twelve loaves of bread were prepared before every Sabbath as part of the meal-offering to God. The baker did not usually understand the rabbi, and probably did not understand him now, but when he heard about the loaves of bread his heart leaped with joy. "At last," he said to himself, "here is something that even I can do for God. I can bake twelve loaves of bread for Him every Sabbath. This will be my gift to Him."

All of the following week the baker worked to save his best flour, and on Friday morning he prepared twelve golden loaves of bread. He wrapped them all up in a white tablecloth and took them to the synagogue. Looking around to make sure that no one else was about, he went up to the holy ark, kissed the curtain in front of the Torah scrolls, and said, "Dear God, I bring You twelve loaves of bread, because the rabbi said You like special bread on the Sabbath. I leave them for You here in the ark where You can find them." He opened the ark, put the loaves neatly inside, closed the ark, kissed the curtain again, and left the synagogue with his heart singing.

Just after the baker left, the caretaker of the synagogue came in with his broom, unaware of what had just happened, sweeping the floor and talking to God. "Dear Lord," he said, "You know I love working here in Your house. It is an honor to sweep the floor for Your sake. But they pay me so little, and my children are hungry. I know You can work miracles. I need a miracle now. Dear Lord, help me." In his distraction the caretaker hardly noticed that he was sweeping in front of the holy ark. Suddenly he smelled the heady fragrance of freshly baked bread! He opened the ark: he could not believe it. God had heard his plea! God had worked a miracle! Twelve loaves, enough to feed his family for a week! With trembling hands he took out the bread, and like the baker, he too kissed the curtain and departed the synagogue in a state of euphoria.

The next morning at Sabbath services, when the rabbi opened the ark to remove the Torah scroll, the baker saw that the loaves were gone. How can words describe his joy! To think that God had accepted his humble gift!

So the next week the baker returned to the synagogue at the very same time and placed twelve new loaves in the ark. A few minutes later the caretaker arrived and once again began sweeping the floor and praying for help, and sure enough when he opened the ark, there were the twelve golden loaves to feed his family. This went on for weeks. It went on for months. The baker would put the bread in the ark, and the caretaker would take it out. Both of them believed that they were witnessing a miracle.

Until one Friday morning, when the inevitable happened: the baker was late to the synagogue. When he arrived, there was the caretaker in front of the open ark, vainly searching for the loaves of bread that had yet to be delivered. As the caretaker turned away from the ark in despair, he saw the baker standing in the doorway holding the tablecloth with the loaves inside. Their eyes met, and at once they both understood what had transpired all of this time. There was no miracle after all.

Or was there? True, it was not the kind of miracle like the one at the Red Sea. It was not the kind of supernatural event that compels belief. But it was the kind of miracle that can still happen: if, like the baker and the caretaker, our love for God is real; if, like them, we feel His presence in the goodness we know and the kindness we do.

It is not always miracles that create faith. Sometimes it is faith that creates miracles.

THE MESSIAH

A STORY IS TOLD about a pious Jew who was very earnest about the commandment to await every day the messiah's arrival. He hired a watchman to wait at the gate of the village, just in case the messiah should show up there. After several years of waiting, the watchman came to complain of the low wages. "True," said the pious man, "the wages are low, but you must admit, the work is steady." He had a point. The Jews have been awaiting the messiah for more than two thousand years, and they are still waiting.

A long time ago, the revered Rabbi Akiba thought that the warrior Bar Kokhba was the anointed one. Akiba's disciples believed it too, at least until Bar Kokhba was defeated by the legions of Rome. Similar claims were made for various contemporaries—including a rabbi and healer from Nazareth—but the Romans killed them all, and the world was still as it was. In the Middle Ages, the prophet Elijah was rumored to have announced the messiah in the streets of Salonika. About the same time, other messiahs were proclaimed in Baghdad, Constantinople, Avila, and Fez. More recent centuries have witnessed new disappointments: Shabbetai Zevi in the seventeenth century, Jacob Frank in the eighteenth. But since human history has not yet ended, and God's kingdom has not yet come, the Jewish people has concluded that the true messiah has yet to make an appearance.

The Jewish sages never stopped looking for him. They searched everywhere for signs of the messianic era, and their deductions were often quite specific. In the Talmud, for instance, it says that there will be a seven-year cycle before the great day comes: the first year will see unusual rainfall; the second year, hunger; the third, famine; the fourth, a remission; the fifth, great plenty; the sixth, sounds from heaven; and the seventh, warfare. Speculations of this kind were commonplace among Jews throughout the Middle Ages. Sometimes the proposed dates coincided with great upheavals in the world or violent persecutions, like the attacks of the Crusaders, the years of the Black Death, or the Ukrainian pogroms. In the twentieth century messianic arithmetic was still attested. During the darkest years of all, in the Warsaw ghetto, many sources document a widespread belief that the messiah would come in the Jewish year 5700, corresponding to the secular years 1939–40, the height of the Third Reich. Of all the messianic predictions, surely this was the most sadly mistaken.

But Jewish faith is resilient, and hope is always reborn. I too confess to dreaming of the messiah, only with this difference: I wonder if I might not already have seen him. If this seems a bit unlikely, consider this teaching from the Talmud: How is the messiah like a scorpion? He comes upon you unawares.

The first time it happened, my son Jesse and I were walking one evening on a crowded city sidewalk. We threaded our way through the traffic and finally stopped at a pizza stand. As Jesse was eating his pizza he said to me, "Did you see that guy?"

"What guy?" I said.

"You know," he said, "that guy lying on the sidewalk."

"What guy? I didn't see anybody."

"He was just lying there," Jesse said. "I thought maybe he was dead, but then he rolled over. He must have been sleeping."

"I didn't see him."

"But Dad, you walked right by him. You almost stepped on him."

I never did see the man there on the sidewalk. It was dark, and I must have been preoccupied, or perhaps too accepting of the sight of misery, as if a man lying in the street were no more than an extension of the curb. Then again, even if I had seen him, I don't know if I would have done anything else.

But it brought to mind a parable I once heard. There was once a man who fell into utter poverty. He tried and tried again to find work, but in the end he was reduced to begging. One night he was walking down a dark street in the midst of a blizzard. His toes were nearly frozen because he had no boots. His arms and hands were numb because he had no coat. Suddenly he tripped over something at his feet. At first he thought it was a log or a stone. But looking closer, he saw that it was a man lying face down in the snow. He did not seem to be breathing. The beggar could not help noticing that this man was wearing a warm coat and a fine pair of boots. As he stood there in the howling wind, the beggar thought about how cold he was, and how warm he would be in that coat and those boots. He looked around; the street was deserted. No one would ever know if he took them for himself. But he also knew that the man in the snow might still be alive. A fearful war went on inside his heart . . . until, from somewhere even deeper within, he knew what he must do. He lifted the man from the snow and carried him to shelter, and indeed the man was still breathing, and his life was saved. But that is not the end of the parable.

The man in the snow was not just anyone. He had placed himself in the beggar's path on purpose. This was his way of measuring our readiness for the final deliverance. Now he said to the beggar: "By your act of kindness, of mercy, and of righteousness, you have brought the messiah to the threshold. Now I will go lay down in the street again. I will wait for the final deed of kindness, for one more act of mercy, to proclaim the kingdom of God."

Now, when I recall that night on the sidewalk and the man I nearly stepped on, I wonder: did I miss my chance?

The messiah, says the Talmud, comes upon you unawares. It happened again, this time in New York City. I was carrying my luggage through Grand Central Station. As always in that place, everything except the walls was in motion, and everyone was in a hurry. In Grand Central, no one stops for long. It is rare, in my experience, for people even to look at one another. But there are corners of the station where some people do stop, sometimes for the last time. The homeless, the hopeless, the helpless, the psychotic—they camp out there, especially on cold nights, trying to keep warm, at least until they are evicted. This is not to sentimentalize: these people are not always the gentlest souls. It can be frightening to walk through there, with the dread of confrontation or even assault, the terrible sight of desperation, the incontinence, the smell. Experienced commuters, as I have since learned, avoid these corners of Grand Central. Once I found myself in one, I did what most New Yorkers learn to do: I walked fast, with a mission, and I aimed my eyes straight ahead.

I was just about to exit the station when I saw a solitary man sitting against the wall. He was calling out something: "Please, please, please. . . . " He looked as bedraggled and forlorn as anyone would who finds himself sitting on the floor of a train station, holding a sign for passersby to notice and a bowl for their coins of pity. But the sign he was holding was different. It didn't say anything about needing food, or shelter, or train fare. His sign said only: "Everything that smells is not trash." That was all it said.

But that is a lot to say.

One day, the Talmud teaches, the prophet Elijah appeared to one of the Jewish sages, and since Elijah is supposed to know, the sage asked him: "When will the messiah come?"

"Go and ask him yourself," Elijah replied.

"And where will I find him?"

"At the gates of the city," said Elijah.

"But how will I recognize him?"

"Look among the poor and the lepers. Look among the wretched and the outcast. You'll find him."

Now I am wondering if the messiah is still there, calling out for our pity, and holding up a sign saying, "Everything that smells is not trash."

The truth is that the messiah has always been here. He comes upon us unawares. He lies crumpled on the streets where we walk. He cries out to us from the dark corner of a train station. But we have avoided him. We have turned away from him. We have stepped right over him. And this is also true: if we treated every unfortunate person as if he were the messiah, it wouldn't matter whether he was or not.

Here on this earth, we may not recognize him. But in paradise, it is said, we will know the messiah. For there we will realize that we have seen him all our lives, in the faces of everyone we ever helped, and in the eyes of everyone we ever loved.